Three Hundred Authenticated Miracles of Muhammad (p.b.u.h.)

Three Hundred Authenticated Miracles of Muhammad (p.b.u.h)

Compiled By
BADR AZIMABADI

ADAM PUBLISHERS & DISTRIBUTORS
New Delhi-110002

Adam Publishers & Distributors

Exporters & Importers

1542, Pataudi House, Daryagunj, New Delhi-2

Ph.: (O) 23282550, 23284740, 23267510

Fax.: 23267510 (R) 95120-2413957

E_mail : apd@bol.net.in

www.adambooks.com

Edition - 2005

ISBN 81-7435-049-7

Price

Printed & Bound In India

Published by

S. Sajid Ali For

Adam Publishers & Distributors

1542, Pataudi House, Daryagunj, New Delhi-2

PUBLISHER'S NOTE

Miracles are essentially the "Signs of Allah shown to whomsoever He like. The Last Prophet's abiding "sign" for all time to come is the Qur'an, each verse of which is termed as "sign" (Ayat). More than once the Qur'an itself threw an open challenge to the proud Arab stylists to match it with their own composition in diction and import. But that challenge has remained unaccepted.

When a miracle takes place, that by itself can not be a direct evidence of prophethood of the person who exhibits the miracle. However, a miracle impresses people with the fact that the person has the spiritual power needed for the showing of the miracle and that he must be true in his claim of prophethood. Moreover, it has been understood, through the ages, that a prophet always has some ultra-natural powers. Therefore, whenever a claim of prophethood has been put forward, people have demanded a show of miracles. In this way, a miracle is a psychological sign of prophethood.

This book has the unique distinction of making the most comprehensive and systematic approach to the subject. It tries to establish the supermacy of the spiritual world over the material one, for the prophets show to the world acts and deeds which are not explainable in terms of worldly thought and logic.

FOREWORD

Miracles are the signs of Allah, the Exalted. These are beyond human comprehension, experience and observation. These events and incidents transcend this material world of ours. Our spiritual world is kept intact and systematic as this world is regulated under precise laws. As we see night following the day, the sun and the moon moving on their orbits and seasons repeating themselves regularly, so we have in our spiritual world, light and darkness, spring and autumn.

Prophets can not perform miracles of their own. Every such act of his is an act of Allah, the Almighty. It is generally exhibited by Allah through the prophet.

Just as there are a number of things and happenings of which we do not know reasons, similarly we do not know how prophet comes to the world at a certain time, and how he is able to exhibit super-natural or ultra-natural events and incidents. The prophet sees and knows many things which we do not see or know of.

Although the real miracle lies in the very existence of the prophet, in his message and in the light of his acts, yet there are many who are not able to read these divinely given signs and they desire the exhibition of material signs which are, at last, shown them.

Since Prophet Muhammad (p.b.u.h) was the last of the prophets and entrusted with teachings for the whole of mankind, he was also given miracles aiming at all mankind. While his behaviour and habits were themselves miraculous, so was the Book entrusted to him; his spiritual powers, his "Miraj", his visions of the past and of the future.

During his battles, clear aid through the angels was a prominent feature. The light of his face, the miraculous effect of his words and the compelling force of his morality; all these were of the nature of miracles and had their due effect, and aid him in attaining the goal set for him.

This book is neither the first nor the only one on the subject. But it is certainly the most comprehensive and systematic of all. The basic sources of the book are the Qur'an and Hadith and then the original historical books. Some of them are:

1. Al-Siha Al-Sitta, i.e., the six authentic books of Hadith.
2. Asha-hus Siyar by Abdur Ra'uf Danapuri.
3. Rahmat-ulil-Älamin by Qazi Muhammad Sulaiman Mansurpuri.
4. Siratun Nabi by Allama Shibli Numani and Allamah Syed Sulaiman Nadwi.
5. Nabi-e-Rahmat by Maulana Abul Hasan Ali Nadwi.
6. Al-sira al-Nabawiyyah by Ibn Hisham.
7. Al-Bidaya wal-Nihayah by Ibn Kathir.
8. Al-Kamil fil Tarikh by Ibn Athir.
9. Mohd The Final Messanger.

I hope the readers in general will benefit from this book.

Okhla, New Delhi **_Badr Azimabadi_**

Feburary 1, 1993

INTRODUCTION

A miracle is a marvellous event caused by a supernatural agency, Almighty Allah. The Holy Qur'an uses words (Aayat, Burhan, etc.) which mean 'sign', 'argument', etc., instead of the word 'Mu'jizah' (miracle). These words are really more to the point.

Miracles (signs) have played an integral part in the lives of the prophets. Spirtual forces have always been the main weapon in their hands. They never based their teachings on any material splendour.

Allah, the Almighty has bestowed miracles to the prophets as signs ("Aayat") of their prophethood. The miracles of David, Solomon, Abraham, Moses and Jesus are very famous. These miracles are also mentioned in the Holy Qur'an along with other miracles. There are some other prophets about whom the Holy Qur'an is silent as regards their miracles, but that, of course, does not mean that no miracles were performed by them. Miracles were needed for those prophets who met the greatest opposition, while those who were ordained only to refresh people's memories about what had been brought by earlier prophets did not need the help of their own miracles.

Prophet Muhammad (p.b.u.h.), being the Last Messenger of Allah for the whole of mankind, was given miracles which were aimed at all mankind.

As a matter of fact the number of miracles performed by the Holy Prophet (p.b.u.h.) far exceeds those performed by any other prophet.

The light of his face, the miraculous effect of his words and the compelling force of his morality, all these were of the nature of miracles and had their due effect, and aided him in attaining the goal set for him, that of propagating Islam successfully. His behaviour and habits were themselves miraculous. The Book entrusted to him, his own spritual powers, Mi'raaj, etc., were all miraculous.

CONTENTS

THE MIRACLES OF THE QUR'AN

1. ***The Holy Qur'an as a miracle:***

The Holy Qur'an is the greatest miracle of Allah, the Almighty. He throws a challenge to all the disbelievers of all times by asking them to produce a sura like it if they are truthful.

"And if you are in doubt concerning that We have sent down to Our servant, then produce a Sura like it and call on your helpers as against Allah if you are truthful."(Q. 2:23)

This is a challenge that the whole human race would not be able to produce a verse like that as one finds in the Holy Qur'an.

And in case they fail to accept this challenge, and most certainly they would not be able to do it, they would have to face the fire whose fuel is human beings and stones. The Holy Qur'an says:

"And if you can not do it — and most certainly you would not be able to do it — then guard against the fire whose fuel is human beings and stones; it is prepared for the disbelievers."(Q. 2:24)

2. ***Mi'raaj:- (ascension of the Holy prophet (p.b.u.h.) to heavens:***

'Mi'raaj' took place in Mak'kah. This wonderful event occured a year before the migration of the Holy Prophet (p.b.u.h) from Mak'kah to Madina. Hazrat Jibrail (Gabriel) came at night, met the Holy Prophet (p.b.u.h.) and led him to 'Masjid-ul-Aqsa' in Jerusalem on Buräq (the horse-like animal). The Messenger of Allah met some of the Prophets there and led the prayer. Thereafter Hazrat Jibrail led the Prophet of Islam to ascend to different layers of the heaven where he met some of the exalted Prophets and observed Heaven and Hell. After that the Holy Prophet (p.b.u.h.) went up and up and got access to Allah, the Almighty, who blessed him, issued some guidance and five times 'namaz' (prayer) was made obligatory. After that he descended to Jerusalem and came back to Mak'kah (Mak'kah) safe and sound.

The Holy Qur'an mentions it in the following words:

"Glory be to Him who made His servant go by night from the sacred Mosque to the farthest Mosque whose precincts We have blessed, that We might show him (some) of Our signs. He is the Hearer, the Seer'. (Q. 17:1).

3. ***Splitting of the moon:***

Once the disbelievers of Mak'kah (Mak'kah) asked the Messenger of Allah to prove his prophethood by showing them any sign regarding it. The Holy Prophet (p.b.u.h.) pointed out his finger towards moon and it splitted up into two pieces.

The Holy Qur'an mentions it as under:

"The Hour (of Judgement) is drawing near, and the moon is cleft in two. Yet when they see a sign (the disbelievers) turn their backs and say: 'Strong magic!" (Q. 54:1)

However, the disbelievers rejected the event as magic.

4. ***Victory of Roman Empire over the Persians:***

The Pagan Quraish of Mak'kah (Mak'kah) rejoiced at the overthrow of Rome by Persia. They were pro-Persian, and in their heart of hearts they hoped that the nascent movement of Islam, which at that time was, from a worldly point of view, very weak and helpless, would also collapse under their persecution. But they misread the true signs of the times. They are told here that they would soon be disillusioned in both their calculations, and it actually so happened at the battle of Issus in 622 (the year of Hijrat) and in 624, when Heraclius carried his campaign into the heart of Persia and the Mak'kan (Mak'kahn) Quraish were beaten off at Badr.

The Battle of Badr (2 A.H = 624 A.D.) was a real time of rejoicing for the Believers and a time of disillusionment for the arrogant Quraish, who thought that they could crush the whole movement of Islam in Madina as they had tried to do in Mak'kah (Mak'kah), but they were signally repulsed.

The Holy Qur'an mentions this event as under:

"Alif Lam mim. The Roman Empire has been defeated in a neighbouring land. But after their defeat they shall themselves gain victory within a few years. Allah's is the command before and after. On that day believers will rejoice in Allah's help. He gives victory to whom He will. He is the Mighty one, the Merciful." (Q 30:1).

5. ***Flights of Birds over Abraha's army:***

Abraha was the Abyssinian governor or viceroy. Intoxicated with power and fired by religious fanaticism, he led a big expedition against Mak'kah, intending to destroy the Ka'ba. He had elephants in his train. But his sacrilegious intentions were defeated by a miracle. No defence was offered by the custodians of the Ka'aba as the army was too strong for them, but it was believed that a shower of stones, thrown by flocks of birds, destroyed the invading army almost to a man. The stones produced sores and pustules on the skin, which spread like a pestilence.

The Holy Qur'an mentions this event as under:

"Have you not seen how Allah dealt with the companions of the Elephant? Did He not foil their treacherous plan? And He sent against them Flights of Birds which pelted them with baked clay, so that they became like plants cropped by cattle?" (Q. 105).

6. ***Sharah Sadr (the expansion of the chest):***

The breast is symbolically the seat of knowledge and the highest feelings of love and affection, the treasure-house in which are stored the jewels of that quality of human character which approaches nearest to the divine. The Holy Prophet's human nature had been purified, expanded, and elevated, so that he became a Mercy to all Creation. Such a nature could afford to ignore the lower motives of ordinary humanity which caused shameful attacks to be made on him. Its strength and courage could also bear the burden of the galling work which it had to do in denouncing sin, subduing it, and protecting God's creatures from its oppression.

The Holy Qur'an describes this event in the following words:

"Have we not expanded your breast and relieved you of the burden which weighed down your back? Have We not given you high renown?" (Q.94: 1-4).

7. ***Conspiracy of Quraish to murder the Holy Prophet (p.b.u.h.) exposed:***

The plots against the Holy Prophet (p.b.u.h.) in Mak'kah aimed at three things. They were not only foiled, but God's wonderful working turned the tables and brought good out of evil each time.

(1). They tried to hold the Apostle in subjection in Mak'kah by putting pressure on his uncles, relatives, and friends. But the more they persecuted, the more the little Muslim community grew in faith and numbers.

(2). They tried to injure and slay him. But the wonderful example of his humanity, perseverence, and fearlessness furthered the cause of Islam.

(3). They tried to get him and his companions out of their homes. But they found a new home in Madina, from which they eventually reconquered not only Mak'kah, but Arabia and the whole world.

Allah, the Almighty says in the Holy Qur'an:

"And (remember) how the unbelievers plotted against you. They sought to take you captive or have you killed or banished.

They plotted but Allah plotted also. But the best of planners is Allah." (Q.8:30)

8. ***Seeing of the Holy Prophet (in dream) the number of unbelievers much less than their actual number on the occasion of the Battle of Badr:***

The Muslim army, though they knew their worldly disadvantage, did not realise the full odds against them. The Mak'kans came exulting in any case, and they despised the contemptible little force opposed to them. Even though they thought the Muslim force was twice as great as it was, still that number was contemptible, when taken with its poor equipment. Both these psychological mistakes subserved the main plan, which was to bring the matter to a decisive issue, whether the Pagans of Mak'kah were to continue their arrogant oppression, or the religion of God was to be established in freedom and honour.

"And (remember) when Allah made them appear to you in a dream as a small band. Had He showed them to you as a great army, your courage would have failed you and you would have quarrelled over the affair. But this Allah spared you. He knows what is in the hearts." (Q. 8:44).

9. This refers to the battle of Badr in Ramadhan in the second year of the Hijra. The little exiled community of Makkan Muslims, with their friends in Madina, had organised themselves into a God-fearing community, but were constantly in danger of being attacked by their pagan enemies of Mak'kah, in alliance with some of the disaffected elements (Jews and Hypocrites) in or near Madina itself. The design of the Mak'kans was to gather all the resources they could, and with an overwhelming force, to crush and annihilate Muhammad (p.b.u.h.) and his party. To this end Abu Sufyan was leading a richely-laden carvan from Syria to Mak'kah. He called for armed aid from Mak'kah. The battle was fought in the plain of Badr, about 50 miles south-west of Madina. The Muslim force consisted of only about 313 men, mostly unarmed, but they were led by Muhammad (p.b.u.h.), and they were fighting for their Faith. The Makkan army, well-armed and well-eqipped, numbered over a thousand and had among its leaders some of the most experienced warriors of Arabia, including Abu Jahl, the inveterate foe and persecutor of Islam. Against all odds the Muslims won a brilliant victory, and many of the enemy leaders, including Abu Jahl, were killed.

It was impossible, without the miraculous aid of Allah, for such a small and ill-eqipped force as was the Muslim band, to defeat the large and well-found force of the enemy. But their firmness, zeal and discipline won them divine aid. Enemy prisoners stated that the enemy ranks saw the Muslim force to be many times larger than it was.

The Holy Qur'an narrates the event as under:

"Indeed, there was sign for you in the two armies which met on the battlefield. One was fighting for the cause of Allah, the other a host of unbelievers. The faithful saw with their very eyes that they were twice their own number. But Allah strengthens with His aid whom He will. Surely in that there was a lesson for the discerning." (Q. 3:13).

10. ***Descending of angels during battles:***

The number of angels, a thousand at Badr and three thousand and five thousand at Uhud, is probably not to be taken literally, but to express a strength at least equal to that of the enemy.

All help comes ultimately from Allah. In special cases it may take special forms to put heart into us, and to fit in with our feelings and our psychology.

Allah, the Almighty says in the Holy Qur'an:

"And when you prayed to your Lord for help. He answered: 'I am sending to your aid a thousand angels in succession.' By this good news Allah sought to reassure your hearts, for victory comes only from Allah; He is Mighty, Wise" (Q.8:9-10).

11. ***Rain before the Battle of Badr:***

Calm (presence of mind) is essential in battle and in all posts of danger. If the mind is too much in a state of excitement, it cannot carry out a well-considered or well-concerted plan. This spirit of calm confidence on the part of the Muslims won against the blustering violence of the Quraish.

The rain was welcome for many reasons:

(1) Water was scarce both for drinking and ablutions;

(2) The Muslim band, without baggage or equipment or comforts, found that their thirst aggravated their fatigue;

(3) The sand was loose, and the rain consolidated it and enabled them "to plant their feet firmly."

"Stain of Satan:" both literally and figuratively. Dirt is physically a symbol of evil, and the Muslims were particular about ablutions before prayer. But the rain also refreshed their spirits and removed any lurking doubts in their minds (suggestions of the Evil One) that victory might be impossible in such adverse circumstances.

The Holy Qur'an narrates as under:

"And when you were overcome by drowsiness, a token of His protection. He sent down water from the sky to cleanse you and to purify you of Satan's filth, to strengthen your hearts and to steady your footsteps."

12. ***Throwing of a handful of dust by the Holy Prophet (p.b.u.h.) at the unbelievers:***

When the Battle of Badr began, the Holy Apostle prayed and threw a handful of dust or sand at the enemy, symbolical of their rushing blindly to their fate. This had a great psychological effect. Every act in the battle is ascribed to Almighty Allah, as it was in His cause, and it was undertaken except by His command.

Numerically the odds against the Muslims were three to one. In other ways they were at a disadvantage: of arms and equipment they had but little, while the enemy were well-found; they were inexperienced, while the Quraish had brought their foremost warriors. In all this there was a test, but the test was accompanied by gracious favour$ of countless value: their Commander was one in whom they had perfect faith, and for whom they were ready to lay down their lives; the rain refreshed them; their spirit was unshaken; and they were fighting in Allah's cause. Thus the trial or test became itself a blessing.

The Holy Qur'an describes it as under:

"It was not you, but Allah, who slew them. It was not you who threw (dust) at them: Allah threw at them so that He might richly reward the faithful. He is Hearing, Knowing." (Q.8:17).

13. ***Dust-storm during the Battle of the Trench:***

In the Battle of the Trench, the enemies of Islam came with a force of ten to twelve thousand fighting men, an unprecedented army for that time and country.

After a close investment of two to four weeks, during which the enemy were disheartened by their ill success, there was a piercing blast of the cold east wind. It was a severe winter, and February can be a very cold month in Madina, which is about 3,000 ft. above the sea-level. The enemy's tents were torn up, their fires were extinguished, the sand and rain beat in their faces, and they were terrified by the portents against them. They had already wellnigh fallen out amongst themselves, and beating a hasty retreat, they melted away. The Madina fighting strength was no more than 3,000 and the Jewish tribe of the Banu Quraiza who were in their midst was a source of weakness as they were treacherously intriguing with the enemy. And further there were the Hypocrites. But there were hidden forces that helped the Muslims. Besides the forces of nature there were moral forces — mutual bickerings and distrust in the enemy camp, and on the other side, perfect discipline among the real Muslims, and the superb leadership of the Holy Prophet (p.b.u.h.).

Almighty Allah sees everything. Therefore we may conclude that the discipline and moral fervour of the Muslims, as well as the enemy's insincerities, intrigues, and reliance on brute force, were all contributory causes to repulse, under Allah's dispensation. There were many hidden causes which neither party saw clearly.

The Holy Qur'an describes this event in the following words:

"Believers, remember Allah's favour to you when there came against you hosts. We unleashed against them a wind and soldiers you could not see. Allah saw all that you were doing." (Q.33:9).

14. ***Allah's help in the Battle of Hunain:***

Hunain is a valley in the mountainous country between Mak'kah and Taif. Immediately after the conquest of Mak'kah (A.H.8), the pagan idolators, who were surprised and chagrined at the wonderful reception which Islam was receiving, orgainised a great gathering near Taif to concert plans for attacking the Apostle. The Hawazin and the Thaqif tribes took the lead and prepared a great expedition for Mak'kah, boasting of their strength and military skill. There was on the other hand a wave of confident enthusiasm among the Muslims at Mak'kah, in which the new Muslims joined. The enemy forces numbered about 4,000 but the Muslim force reached a total of ten or twelve thousand, as every one wished to join. The battle was joined at Hunain.

For the first time the Muslims had at Hunain tremendous odds in their favour. But this itself constituted a danger. Many in their ranks had more enthusiasm than wisdom, more a spirit of their cause. The enemy had the advantage of knowing the ground throughly. They laid an ambush in which the advance guard of the Muslim force was caught. The country is hilly, in which the enemy concealed himself. As soon as the Muslim vanguard entered the Hunain valley, the enemy fell upon them with fury and caused havoc with their arrows from their places of concealment. In such ground the numbers of the Muslims were themselves a disadvantage. Many were slain, and many turned back in confusion and retreat. But the Apostle, as ever, was calm in his wisdom and faith. He rallied the forces and inflicted the most crushing defeat on the enemy.

The Apostle never approved of over-weening confidence, or reliance merely upon human strength, or human resources or numbers. In the hour of danger and seeming disaster, he was perfectly calm, and with cool courage relied upon the help of Allah, whose standard he carried. His calmness inspired all around him, and stopped the rout of those who had turned their backs. It was with Allah's help that they won, and their victory was complete. They followed it up with an energetic pursuit of the enemies, capturing their camps, their flocks and herds, and their families, whom they had boastfully brought with them in expectation of an easy victory.

The Holy Qur'an narrates the whole event as under:

"Assuredly Allah did help you in many battlefields and on the day of Hunain: Behold! your great numbers elated you, but they availed you naught: the land, for all that it is wide, did constrain you, and you turned back in retreat.

"But Allah did pour His calm on the Apostle and on the Believers and sent down forces which you saw not: He punished the Unbelievers: thus does He reward those without Faith." (Q9: 25-26).

15. ***Exposition of the Conspiracy of Banu Na.dir:***

In the life-time of Apostle it happened again and again to enemies of Islam streched out their hands against the Apostle, his people, and his teaching. The odds were, from a worldly point of view, in their favour, but their hands were rendered inert and powerless because they were fighting against the Truth of Allah, the Almighty.

Once the Holy Prophet (p.b.u.h.) with ten persons, went to Banu Na.dir to arrive at some understanding on the mode of paying blood money for the two persons killed by Hazrat Amr bin Umayyah. A part of the money had to be contributed by Banu Na.dir as well. They received the Apostle with a show of friendship and asked him to sit down below a high wall. They apparently agreed to pay the money but secretly contrived a person, Amr bin Jahash (a Jew), to climb up the top of the wall and throw a big stone on the Holy Prophet (p.b.u.h.). The Apostle perceived this and got up from his place and returned to Madina immediately without saying a single word.

The Holy Qur'an describes the event as under:

"O believers, remember the favour which Allah bestowed upon you when certain people were about to stretch their hands towards you, but He restrained them. Have fear of Allah. In Allah let the faithful put their trust." (Q. 5:12).

16. ***Promise of "Khilafat." (i.e., inheritance of the land):***

Three things are promised to those who have faith and obey Allah's law:

(1) That they will inherit power and authority in the land, for not any selfish purpose of theirs nor by way of favouritism, but in order that they may maintain Allah's law;

(2) That the Religion of Right, which Allah has chosen for them, will be openly established, and will suppress all wrong and oppression;

(3) That the righteous will live in peace and security, instead of having to suffer persecution, or leave their hearths and homes for the cause of Allah, or practise the rites of their Faith in secret.

The Muslims then lived in a state of great suspense and danger. The security and authority they were promised came to them subsequently in abundant measure. The promise was totally fulfilled during the period of pious Caliphs.

The Holy Qur'an refers to this promise as under:

"Allah has promised those among you who believe and work righteous deeds, that He will, of a surety, grant them in the land, inheritance (of power), as He granted it to those before them; that He will establish in authority their religion — the one which He has chosen for them; and that He will change (their state), after the fear in which they (lived), to one of security and peace: 'They will worship Me (alone) and not associate aught with Me! If any do reject Faith after this, they are rebellious and wicked." (Q. 24:55).

17. ***Promise of the victory over un-believers of Mak'kah:***

The Muslims faithfully observed the terms of the treaty of Hudaibiya. By this Treaty the Mak'kan Quraiṣh, after many years of unrelenting conflict with Islam, at length recognised Islam, as an equal power with themselves. In reality the door was then opened for the free spread throughout Arabia and thence through the world.

The Mak'kans broke the peace in the attack which one of their allied tribes (the Banu Bakr) made on the Muslim Ban-u Khuza' (who were in alliance with the Prophet), but this led to the conquest of Mak'kan and sweeping away of autocracy.

The Holy Qur'an describes the event in the following words:

"Verily We have given you a manifest victory." (Q.48:1).

18. ***Prophecy of the sad demise of the Holy Prophet (p.b.u.h.):***

The Holy Prophet (p.b.u.h.) migrated from Mak'kah to Madina, a hunted and persecuted man. In Madina all the forces of truth and their confederates to destroy him and his community recoiled on their own hands. Gradually all the outlying parts of Arabia ranged themselves round his standard, and the bloodless conquest of Mak'kah was the crown and prize of his patience and constant endeavour. After that, whole tribes and tracts of country gave their adhesion to him collectively, and before his earthly ministry was finished, the soil was prepared for the conquest of the wide world for Islam.

The task assigned to the Holy Prophet (p.b.u.h.) was over. Hence the sad demise of the Apostle logically drew near. Sura 'Al-Nasr' of the Holy Qur'an revealed the departure of the Holy Prophet (p.b.u.h.) which is mentioned as under:

"When Allah's help and victory come, and you see men embrace His religion in multitudes, celebrate the praise of your Lord and seek His pardon. He is ever disposed to mercy." (Q. 110: 1-3)

19. ***The Prophet's Illiteracy:***

Although the Holy Prophet (p.b.u.h.) was unlettered, the pagans used to propagate that the Qur'an was penned by him. They knew very well that the Apostle could not have acquired knowledge from any other human being as all around him there was darkness and ignorance and there was no source for him from which he could acquire learning and knowledge.

Allah, the Almighty, has claimed in the Qur'an as under:

"Never have you (O 'Muhammad) read a book before this, nor have you ever transcribed one with your right hand. Had you done either of these, the unbelievers might have doubted." (Q. 29:48).

20. ***Jinn:***

'Jinn' was that which is hidden. The Jinns are hidden from human sight, and this concept is common to almost all religions. Even today, experiences with 'spirits' baffle the scientists and philosophers and materialists. The Bible is full of Hazrat Isa's miracles of ridding human beings of the evil influence of Jinns and spirits.

The Holy Qur'an says:

"We created man from dry clay, from black moulded loam, before him the jinn from smokeless fire." (Q. 15:26).

21. ***Frequency of Shahab-i-Saaqib:-***

At the time of the Prophet's ordainment, when the jinns found their way to heaven barred, it was seen that there was a great increase in the number of 'Shahaab' (meteorites) to prevent their access.

The Holy Qur'an describes this phenomenon as under:

"Say: 'it is revealed to me that a party of jinn listened to (Allah's revelations) and said: "We have heard a wondrous Qur'an" (Q.72:1).

22. ***A Mystifying Unrest:***

The Holy Prophet (p.b.u.h.) was now approaching his fortieth year. He felt a mystifying internal unrest, yet he did not know the reason for it. He was himself not aware what the inexplicable perplexity meant to him; nor did the idea that God was about to honour him with revelation and prophethood ever cross his mind. This was how the Prophet (p.b.u.h.) felt, as has been attested by Almighty Allah:

"And thus We have inspired you with a spirit of Our will when you knew nothing of faith or scripture, and made it a light whereby We guide those of Our servants whom We please. (Q. 42:52).

23. ***Mercy from Lord:***

The inability of the Holy Prophet (p.b.u.h.) to know the reason for his internal unrest has been evinced in the following words:-

"You never hoped that this Book would be sent to you except as mercy from your Lord. Therefore give no help to the unbelievers." (Q. 28:86).

24. ***King Najashi (Negus) Weeps Bitterly:***

The news that the Muslims were living in peace in Abyssinia reached Mak'kah and the faces of the Quraishiite were clouded over. They sent their emissaries, laden with the choicest presents of Mak'kah for the Negus, his nobles and chiefs, to get the exiles back from Abyssinia. The agents of the Quraish first bribed the courtiers of the Negus and thereafter they took their presents to the Negus and lodged a strong complaint against the Muslims.

The king summoned the Muslims to his court where his bishops were present, and asked the Muslims, "What is that religion for which you have forsaken your people, and neither accepted my religion nor any other?"

Thereupon J'afar bin Abu Talib (r.a.), cousin of the Prophet (p.b.u.h.), explained to the king about Islam.

Negus listened patiently to J'afar. Then he asked J'afar if he had something brought by his Prophet from God.

J'afar replied in the affirmative. Negus asked him to recite the same. Thereupon J'afar recited the opening Verses of 'Sura Maryam.' Negus wept until his beard was wet; the bishops wept until their scrolls were wet with their tears.

25. ***'Umar Embraces Islam:***

Umar was one of the nobles of the Quraish. He was feared and respected by all. The Apostle wished that he should accept Islam.

Fatima bint al-Khattab, the sister of 'Umar, accepted Islam and shortly thereafter her husband' Sa'id b. Zayd, too followed suit. But both kept it a closely guarded secret.

"One day 'Umar planned to murder the Apostle. He took his

sword and left in search of the Apostle. Nu'aymb. 'Abdullah met him in the way and asked, "Umar, where are you going?"

"I seek Muhammad, was Umar's reply, "and I will slay him..."

"Better far would it not be to set your own family in order?"

'Umar was taken aback. He asked, "and who are they in my family?"

Nu'aym replied, "Your brother-in-law and cousin Sa'id b. Zayd and your sister Fatima. They have given faith to Muhammad (p.b.u.h.) and accepted his religion.

'Umar forthwith hurried on to the house of his sister. Khabbab was at that time reading the "Sura TaHa" to the couple from a manuscript he had with him.

'Umar threw himself upon his brother-in-law, Fatima rushed in to save her husband but 'Umar struck her hard and wounded her.

'Umar saw the blood flowing from the wound he had inflicted on his sister. His anger gave place to shame. Cooled down, he asked for the manuscript which he had heard Khabbab reading. She said to him firmly, 'My brother, you are unclean because of your polytheism, and only the pure can touch it." Umar rose and took a bath. His sister then gave him the pages on which 'Sura Ta Ha' was written. He had read only a few lines when he exclaimed in amazement, 'How noble and sublime is this speech!"

Thereafter 'Umar asked khabbab to lead him to the Apostle so that he might accept Islam.

In short, 'Umar approached the Apostle and submitted, "O Messenger of Allah, I have come to attest my faith in Allah and His Apostle and what he has brought from Allah."

26. ***Sparkling Symphony of the Qur'an:***

Tufayal b. 'Amr al-Dausi was a noted poet of Arabia. When he came to Mak'kah, some of the Quraish warned him against meeting the Apostle.

Tufayal relates: "By God, they were so insistent that I decided not to listen or speak to him. I went so far to stuff cotten in my ears before going to the holy mosque. Suddenly, my eyes met the Apostle who was offering prayer near me. I stood by his side and thus God caused me to hear something of his speech. It was beautiful and noble. I thought, I am a poet and the connoisseur for nothing good or evil in a speech can elude me. Why should anything prevent me from listening to this speech? If it is good I shall accept it; if bad, I shall reject it."

He met the Apostle at his house where he invited him to accept Islam and recited the Qur'an to him. Tufayl accepted Islam and went back to his tribe determined to preach the faith of God.

27. ***Recital of the Qur'an:***

Hazrat Abu Bakr (R.A.) used to pray within his house. Not being satisfied with it, he selected a place in the courtyard of his house where he started offering prayers and reciting the Qur'an. Abu Bakr was tender-hearted and when he recited the Qur'an, shedding tears all the while, youths, slaves and women used to gather round him listening to his recitation.

28. ***Conspiracy Against the Apostle:***

Migration of the Muslims to Madina frightened the Mak'kans out of their wits. They very soon realised that the Apostle had already established a base with a large number of adherants in a foreign territory beyond their reach and if he were also to join them there, then they would be rendered helpless, deprived of all authority over him. They held a council in Dar al-Nadwa where all the chiefs of the Quraish assembled to delibrate how to solve the problem.

They debated the various suggestions and ultimately decided unanimously that each clan should provide a young, courageous and blue-blooded warrior so that all of them fall upon Muhammad (p.b.u.h.) jointly to kill him. Thus, the responsibility of shedding his blood would lie equally on all the clans.

But the Apostle was warned of their wicked plan by the All-Knowing God; he asked 'Ali to lie on his bed and to wrap himself in his mantle. He also told 'Ali that no harm would come to him.

The murderous band stood outside the Apostle's house with drawn scimitars in their hands, in readiness to attack the Prophet (p.b.u.h.). The Apostle of Allah came out and took a handful of dust. Almighty Allah instantly took away their sight and the Apostle went through their ranks, sprinkling the dust over their heads and reciting the Sura Yasin. "We have set a barrier before them and a barrier behind them and covered them over, so that they cannot see." (Q. 36:9).

29. ***The Celestial Assistance:***

At the time of the migration when the Holy Prophet (p.b.u.h.) and Hazrat Abu Bakr entered the cave on Mt. Thawr, a spider spinned its web across the mouth of the cave on a bush at the entrance, concealing the Apostle from those who might look into it. Thereafter came two doves which fluttered over the cave for sometime and then sat down to lay eggs there — Allah's are the forces of the heavens and the earth. Allah is Mighty and Wise." (Q. 48:7).

30. ***Most Critical Moment:***

When the Holy Prophet (p.b.u.h.) and Hazrat Abu Bakr were on his way to Madina the Qurayshi'ite horsemen on the look out for the two fugitives galloping over the desert came to the cave where the two had crouched. This was the most critical moment of human history. The world was holding its breath in suspense. The pursuers who stood on the mouth of the cave had only to look down in the cave, but the web on the mouth of the cave convinced them that nobody could be inside it. It was something miraculous to see how Almighty Allah helped His Apostle.

The Holy Qur'an refers to this event as under:-

"In the cave, he said to his companion: 'Do not despair. Allah is with us." Allah caused His peace to descend upon him and sent to his aid invisible warriors, so that he routed the unbelievers and exalted the word of Allah. Allah is Mighty, Wise." (Q.9:40).

31. ***A prediction:-***

The Apostle of Allah had been driven out of his homeland, the enemy on the look out for him was after his blood, but his mind's eye was calling up the day when his followers would be trampling the realms of Caesars and Chosroes. In those adverse circumstances, the darkest hour of his life, he made a prediction of the bright times ahead. To Suraqa he said, "Suraqa, how would you feel when you would put on Chosroes' bracelets?"

Almighty Allah has indeed promised succour and victory and prosperity to His Apostle and the triumphant ascendancy of His Religion of Truth.

"It is he who has sent His apostle with the guidance and the Religion of Truth, to make it triumphant over all religions, however much the disbelievers may dislike it." (Q. 9:33).

32. ***To unite unbelievers on one Faith:***

The new home (Madina) of the emigrees was dissimilar in many respects from the town (Mak'kah) they had left. It was comparatively smaller from the former but the society there was more complex in comparison to the social life of Mak'kah. The Apostle was, therefore, expected to come across problems of a different nature. The town was peopled by men subscribing to different religions with dissimilar social codes and customs and having divergent cultural patterns. The task now presented to him was how to overcome the difficulties arising out of a hetrogeneous community and how to unite them on one creed and faith. It was a difficult assignment which could be accomplished only by a prophet, commissioned and blest by Allah with wisdom, foresight, firmness of purpose and capacity to blend the conflicting ideas and ideals into a new concept which could usher the dying humanity into a new brave world. And above all, the saviour had to have a loveable personality. How very correctly has Allah set forth the service rendered by that benefactor of the human race.

"If you had given away all the riches of the earth, you could not have so united them; but Allah has united them. He is Mighty, Wise." (Q.8:63).

33. ***Helplessness of Islam in Mak'kah:***

Islam was helpless, harried and harrassed in Mak'kah. None had the power to turn the tide there; nor could anyone think of gaining any advantage by accepting Islam. Giving one's faith to Islam meant that one was prepared to set the whole of Mak'kah at defiance and to risk one's life. Only a man of mettle could take a chance with his life and property, future and prosperity. In Mak'kah there were not two powers equally poised; the heathens were strong and tyrants and the Muslims, weak and oppressed.

On this occasion the Muslims were reminded that they were a small band in Mak'kah; despised and rejected; living in a state of insecurity for their persons, their lives, their property, and those of their dependants; persecuted and exiled away and how by the grace of Allah they found a safe asylum in Madina, how they found friends and helpers, and how at length they gathered strength and numbers enough to defeat the forces of godlessness, injustice and oppression.

This was the situation obtaining in Mak'kah which has been brought out forcefully by the Qur'an in its elegant style:

"And remember how He gave you shelter when you were few in number and considered weak in the land, ever fearing the onslaught of your enemies. He made you strong with His help." (Q. 8:26).

34. *Throwing Fears Into The Hearts of The Unbelievers:*

In the Battle of Badr, the Muslims fought the Mak'kans like a firm, united and disciplined army with the name of Allah on their lips. Up to the moment the Apostle had remained quiet and collected, but now he charged into the ranks of the enemy. None was now braver than he, none dared engage the enemy so closely. Allah, the Almighty now sent down angels from heaven to the succour of the Muslims; the enemy seemed to be giving way to the Muslims and was driven back by the fierce charge of the invisible battlers.

The Holy Qur'an describes the event in the following words:

"And when Allah inspired the angels, (saying): 'I shall be with you. Give courage to the believers, I shall cast terror into the hearts of the infidels. Strikes off their heads, smite the ends of their fingers." (Q.8:12).

35. *Speedy Victory:*

The Treaty of Hudaibiya itself was a "speedy victory": it followed immediately after the 'Bai'at.'

The gain so far seen from the Bai'at and their calm and disciplined behaviour were certainly great; but greater still were to follow in the spiritual sense, in the rapid spread of Islam, in the clearance from the Sacred House of the idolatrous autocracy, and in the universal acceptance of the Message of God in Arabia.

The Holy Qur'an describes it as under:

"He rewarded them with speedy victory; and many gains will they acquire (besides): and Allah is Exalted in Power, Full of Wisdom. (Q.48: 18-19).

36. *Prophecy Regarding Later Victories:*

Prophecy had already been made in the Holy Qur'an regarding later victories of Islam, but we must view them not merely in their political or moral aspect, but chiefly in the rise of Islam as a world power morally and spiritually.

The Holy Qur'an says:

"And other gains (there are), which are not within your power, but which Allah has compassed; and Allah has power over all things." (Q.48:21).

37. *Allah's Bounty Not Confined To One Group:*

Of the prophecies of the Holy Qur'an is that soon after the demise of the Holy Prophet (p.b.u.h.) some people will turn apostate and rebel against the spirit of Islam. The prophecy came true. Mosailma the False pretended to prophetship. he was killed by

Wahshi and Khalid bin Walid crushed the rebellions during the Caliphate of Hazrat Abu Bakr (r.a.)

"The Holy Qur'an says:

"O true believers! If any from among you turn back from his Faith, soon will Allah produce a people whom He will love as they will love Him, — lowly with the Believers, Mighty against the Rejecters, fighting in the way of Allah, and never afraid of the reproaches; (Q.5:57).

38. ***Religion of Truth Shall Overtop all:***

Allah, the Almighty promises that Islam shall overtop all other religions, and so it came to be. Of the most prevalent religions then, the Persian Magiism was foremost, and next to it the Roman Christianism. And in a short period Islam obtained ascendency over them both. The Persian Monarcry was destroyed in a few days and no vestige of it remained; and the Roman Empire was entirely succumbed, and much of their possessions were ceded to Islam.

The Holy Qur'an describes it as under:

"It is He Who has sent His Apostle with Guidance and the Religion of Truth to proclaim it over all religions: and enough is Allah for a Witness." (Q. 48:28).

39. ***Prophecy that Came True:***

The Holy Qur'-an made a prophecy as under:

"Their army shall be routed and put to flight." (Q.54:45)

The above-mentioned prophecy came true in the Battle of Badr when Mak'kan took to their heels from the battle-ground.

40. ***Goodly Reward Or Grievous Penalty:***

Of the prophecies of the Holy Qur'an is the following verse.

The desert Arabs loved fighting and plunder and understood such motives for war. The higher motives seemed to be beyond them. Like ignorant men they attributed petty motives of jealousy if they were kept out of the vulgar circle of fighting for plunder. But they had to be schooled, and they were schooled to higher ideas of discipline, self-sacrifice, and striving hard for a Cause.

While they were reported for their supineness in the march which led to Hudaibiya, where there was danger but not prospect of booty, they were promised, if they learnt discipline, to be allowed to follow the Banner of Islam where there was real fighting with formidable and well-organised armies.

They were told, "You shall go forth to war if you learn discipline, not for booty, but for a great and noble cause. For if your opponents submit to the Cause, there will be no fighting and no booty.

The Holy Qur'an says:

"Say to the desert Arabs who lagged behind: "You shall be summoned (to fight) against a people given to vehement war: then shall you fight, or they shall submit, then if you show obedience, Allah will grant you a goodly reward, but if you turn back as you did before, He will punish you with a grievous Penalty." (Q. 48:16).

The above-mentioned prophecy came true in persian and Byzantine wars.

41. ***Promise To Protect The Prophet (p.b.u.h.):***

Muhammad (p.b.u.h.) had many difficulties to contend with, many enemies and dangers to avoid. This is to assure him that his message was true and from the Almighty Allah. His mission must be fulfilled. And he must — as he did — go forward and proclaim that message and fulfil his mission, trusting to Allah for protection, and unconcerned if people who had lost all sense of right rejected it or threatened him.

The Holy Qur'an describes the above as under:

"And Allah will defend you from men (who mean mischief)." (Q.5:70).

After the revealation of the above verse, the Holy Prophet (p.b.u.h.) relieved his security guards and left himself in the protection of Allah, the Almighty, who kept him safe and sound all his life.

42. ***Faith And Right Remain Unharmed:-***

The logical conclusion to the evolution of religious history is a non-sectarian, non-racial, non-docrinal, universal religion, which Islam claims to be. For Islam is just submission to the will of Allah. This implies (1) Faith, (2) doing right, being an example to do right, and having the power to see that the right prevails, (3) eschewing wrong, being an example to others to eschew wrong, and having power to see that wrong and injustice are defeated. Islam therefore lives, not for itself but for mankind. The People of the Book, if only they had faith would be Muslims, for they have been prepared for Islam. Unfortunately there is unfaith, but it can never harm, those who carry the banner of Faith and Right, which must always be victorious.

The Holy Qur'an refers to it as under:

"They will do you no harm, barring a trifling annoyance; if they come out to fight you, they will show you their backs, and no help shall they get." (Q.3:111).

MIRACLES MENTIONED IN THE BOOKS OF AHADITH

43. ***The opening of the Chest:***

The miracle of "Shaqq-al-Sadr," (the opening of the chest) occured twice during the life of the Holy Prophet (p.b.u.h.):

(1) When he was about 5 years old.

(2) When he was to go on the heavenly journey of "Mi'raj."

On the first occasion the "Satanic part" was taken out from his chest, while on the second occasion when this miracle took place on the occasion of "Isra" or "Miraj", "Knowledge and Wisdom" were put into his heart and the chest was washed with Zam Zam. (Bukhari, Mishkat).

44. ***Greetings ((salam) by Trees and Stones:***

Hazrat Ali bin Abu Talib (r.a.) reports:

"I was coming along with the Holy Prophet (p.b.u.h.) in Mak'kah. No mountain or tree met him but was saying: "As-Salamu 'Alaika Ya Rasul-Allah (peace be on thee, O Messenger of Allah)" (Muslim, Mishkat).

45. ***Movement of Trees:***

Hazrat ibn Abbas (r.a.) reports:

"A Bedouin Arab came to the Messenger of Allah and said, "How shall I know that you are a Prophet?" The Apostle said, "In case this date-tree bear witness that I am the Messenger of Allah." The Bedouin agreed. Then the Apostle called it and the date-tree moved towards the Prophet (p.b.u.h.) and fell down before him. Thereafter the Apostle asked the tree "to go back". Then the tree returned to its place. The Bedouin Arab accepted Islam then and there (Tirmidhi).

46. Once the Holy Prophet (p.b.u.h.) went out to excrete. Jabir (r.a.) accompanied him with a bowl of water. In the field the Apostle searched a fence of trees but could not get any. However, he saw two trees away on the side of the field. He went to one of them and holding its branch said: "With the Commandment of Allah, obey me." The tree came with him. He did similarly with the other tree which also came with him near the former tree. Then he asked them to join together to make a fence. Thereafter he answered his nature's call behind the trees. Afterwards he asked both the trees to go back to their places and they did accordingly. (Muslim).

47. ***Ma'n bin Abd ar-Rahman (r.a.) reports:*** to have heard from his father saying that he asked Martuq who told the Prophet (p.b.u.h.) about the jinn on the night they listened to the Qur'an and he replied, "Your father (Abdullah bin Mas'ud) told me that he said a tree told about them." (Bukhari, Muslim).

48. ***Hazrat Anas (r.a.) reports:***

Hazrat Jibrail came to the Prophet (p.b.u.h.) when he was sitting grieved and smeared with blood as a result of what the Mak'kans had done and said, "Messenger of Allah, would you like me to show you a sign?" The Apostle agreed. Hazrat Jibrail looked at a tree behind him and said, "Call it." The Apostle called and it came and stood in front of him. He then said, "Order it to go back." When he did so, he went back. Thereupon the Messenger of Allah said, "That is enough for me; that is enough for me." (Darimi).

49. ***Hazrat ibn Umar (r.a.) reports:***

Once we were on journey with the Prophet (p.b.u.h.) that a nomadic Arab approached The Messenger of Allah and said to him, "Do you testify that none has the right to be worshipped but Allah alone, who has no partner and that Muhammad is his servant and messenger?"

He replied, "Who will testify to what you say?"

"The mimosa tree," the Apostle said.

"The Prophet (p.b.u.h.) called the tree and it came furrowing the ground and stood before him. The Apostle asked the tree to testify three times. The tree did so and then returned to its site. (Darimi).

50. ***Weeping by a Dead Stem of a Date Tree:***

Hazrat Jabir (r.a.) reports:

Whenever the Holy prophet (p.b.u.h.) delivered his sermon, he used to lean against the (dead) stem of a date tree. When a pulpit was prepared for him, he stood upon it. The date stem cried aloud and wept bitterly till it was about to be split up. The Holy Prophet (p.b.u.h.) got down from his pulpit and patted and embraced. Thereupon it started groaning like a child and became quiet.

51. ***Gushing Out Springs Of Water From Fingers:***

Hazrat Jabir (r.a.) reports:

"On the day of Hudaibiya the people were thirsty and they approached the Apostle for water. The water-vessel had very little water. The Apostle started performing ablution. After that he put his hand into the vessel and water began to pour forth between his fingers like springs. The people drank and performed ablution. They numbered fifteen hundred (Bukhari, Muslim).

52. ***Making a Dry Well Wet:***

Hazrat Al-Bara'b. Azib (r.a.) reports:

On the day of Hudaibiya, we were along with the Apostle. We numbered fourteen hundred. There was a well which we drained leaving not a drop in it. When the Prophet heard of that he came to the well and sat down beside it. He called for a vessel of water and while performing ablution, he rinsed his mouth and made supplication. Then he poured water into the well and asked his companions to leave it for some time. Thereafter they drew water for themselves and their animals until they left. (Bukhari).

53. ***Drawing Water From Water-skins:***

Hazrat Abdur 'Rahman bin Auf quotes Abu-Raja' to have reported from Imran bin Husain:

Once during journey we complained the Prophet (p.b.u.h.) of thirst. He dismounted and called some of us and asked to look for water. They went off and came across a woman riding with a leather water-skin on either side of her. They brought her to the Apostle who asked her to dismount from her camel.

The Prophet (p.b.u.h.) asked for a vessel and poured water into it from the mouths of skins. Then we were asked to draw water. We forty thirsty men drank to our fill and filled every skin and small vessel which we had with us. I swear by Allah that it seemed to us to be fuller than it was when the Apostle began.

54. ***Dry Stream At Tabuk:***

When the Muslims reached Tabuk, they found that the stream there was almost dry. As the Prophet (p.b.u.h.) had instructed them, they waited for the Apostle to arrive. On his arrival, he washed his hands and face with the water available and the water thus used was put back into the stream which then started flowing with water.

55. ***Water In the Empty Vessel:***

Once water flowed from the fingers of the Holy Prophet (p.b.u.h.) when even his own bowl had almost no water in it. He recited something and asked that the water be poured out. Enough was there, and when he withdrew his hand from the vessel, there was still plenty in the vessel.

56. ***Quenching the Thirst of the Companions:***

On one journey, the Holy Prophet (p.b.u.h.) asked Abu Qatadah (r.a.) to preserve the little water that was with him for his (Prophet's) ablution (Wudu). Later, during the journey, the companions were very thirsty. Thereupon the Apostle sent for the preserved water. Abu Qatadah brought the water which was given to the people. All of them got satisfied.

57. ***Water Bubbling out through Fingers:***

On yet another journey, the Holy Prophet (p.b.u.h.) gave Habban (r.a.) some water in a vessel with which the latter did his wudu. After that, the Apostle put his fingers inside the vessel and water started bubbling out through his fingers so that people were invited to perform their wudu with it.

58. ***Similar Incident:***

Hazrat Abdullah bin Masood (r.a.) reports:

Once the Holy Prophet (p.b.u.h.) gave him some water to preserve it with him. He did so. When the companions of the Apostle requested him to provide water for drinking and performing wudu, he asked Abdullah to bring the water preserved by him. He obeyed and the water proved enough for the need.

59. ***Joining of the Broken Bone:***

Hazrat Bara (r.a.) reports:

'Once the Holy Prophet (p.b.u.h.) sent a party to Abu Rafi. Abdullah bin Atik entered his house at night while he was asleep and killed him. Abdullah bin Atik himself reports, "I fixed my sword over his belly till it went out by his back. When I was satisfied that I had killed him, I opened the door and came to a staircase. As I put my feet, I fell down and my leg was fractured. I had it bandaged with my turban. Thereafter I met my companions and appeared before the Apostle. I informed him about the accident. The Holy Prophet (p.b.u.h.) said, 'spread your leg.' I did accordingly. He passed his hand over it and it was cured. I felt as if it had not broken at all." (Bukhari, Mishkat).

60. ***Hazrat Ali Cured:***

On the occasion of the Battle of Khaybar, Hazrat Ali (r.a.) was suffering from ophthalmia. The Holy Prophet (p.b.u.h.) summoned him and applied his spittle to his eyes and prayed for his success. The eyes of Ali were cured in no time.

61. ***Injured Eye Secured:***

When the Mak'kans failed to stop the Muslims from accepting Islam, they lost their mental balance and started persecuting the Faithfuls. One of the victims was Uthman bin Mazun (r.a.).Once he had a heated wrangle with a polytheist who slapped him so hard in the face that he lost an eye. Thereafter he appeared before the Holy Prophet (p.b.u.h.) and narrated the incident. The Apostle put the injured eye at its proper place and it looked so fit and sound as if it was never injured. (Ibn Hisham.).

62. ***Healing of Wound***: During the Battle of Khayber, Hazrat Salmah bin Akwa' received a serious wound on his leg. The people started saying, "Salmah has been wounded." Dejected he came to the

Apostle and showed him his wound. The Merciful Prophet (p.b.u.h.) puffed off therin three breaths and the wound healed up." (Bukhari, Muslim, Mishkat).

63. ***The Victorious Commander:***

After a few unsuccessful charges at Khaybar, the Holy Prophet (p.b.u.h) said, "Tomorrow I will give the standard to a man who loves Allah and His Apostle and he will conquer the fort."

The prophecy of the Holy Prophet (p.b.u.h.) came true and Hazrat Ali (r.a.) conquered the fort.

64. ***Enchantment Done Upon The Prophet (p.b.u.h.):***

Hazrat A'isha (r.a.) reports:

The Messenger of Allah was enchanted, so much so that he conjuctured that he did a thing while he did not do it, so much so that when one day he was near me, he supplicated to Allah and supplicated to Him again. Thereafter he said, "O 'A'isha ! Do you know that Allah revealed to me about what I sought decision from Him ? Two men (angels) came to me; one of them said to his companion, "What is the pain of the man ?" He said, 'He has been enchanted ? The first man (angel) again asked, 'And who enchanted him? The second person (angel) replied, 'Labid bin al-A'sam, the Jew. "The first angel further enquired, 'In what thing?" The second angel said, "In a comb and combed hairs and the spathe of a male palm-tree." The first angel again asked, "Where is it?" The second said, "In the well of Dharwan." The Holy Prophet (p.b.u.h.) went with a party of his companions to the well and said. 'This is the well which was shown to me.' Its water was as it were reddish-brown, a complexion of Henna, and its date trees were as it were the heads of devils. Then they (searched the well and) took (all the things, told by angels) out (of the well) (Bukhari, Muslim, Mishkat).

65. ***Prophecy About The Death Of A Hypocrite:-***

Hazrat Jabir (r.a.) reports:

"The Holy Prophet (p.b.u.h.) was coming back from a journey. When he was nearing Madina, wind began to blow in such a way as it could bury a rider. The Apostle said, "This wind has been sent for the death of a hypocrite." On reaching Madina we came to know that the chief of the hypocrites, Rifa'a bin Darir had died" (Muslim, Mishkat).

66. ***Roasted Flesh Of Goat Informing about The Poison:-***

Hazrat Jabir (r.a.) reports:

A Jewess from Khybar invited the Holy Prophet (p.b.u.h.) on a feast. Shc mixed poison with roasted mutton and served it. The Apostle took a (cooked) arm and ate (a little) therefrom. One of his companions also ate it. "Raise up your hands." exclaimed the Apostle. then he asked the Jewess, "Have you poisioned this mutton?" "Who has informed you?" The Apostle replied, "This (cooked) arm in my hand has informed me." "Yes, she said and added, "I (did it) to know if you are a Prophet, it will never injure you; and if you are not a Prophet, we will get rid of you." Thereupon the Apostle pardoned her. However, his companion died. (Abu Dawud; Darmi, Bukhari).

67. ***Increase In Commodities:***

During the Battle of Trench, when the trench was being dug, there was no food. The Holy Prophet (p.b.u.h.) and his companions were digging the trench day and night without food.

Hazrat Jabir (r.a.)-had a lamb. He slaughtered it and asked his wife to cook the mutton and bake some breads from barly floor. He then came to the Holy Prophet (p.b.u.h.) and invited him on the feast.

Although he had invited him alone, but the Apostle made an announcement and invited all the companions (about 3,000) on the feast. When the Messenger of Allah arrived at his house with his companions, Jabir (r.a.) got embarrassed. However, the Apostle asked him to bring the food. He chanted something and mixed his revered saliva in the food and it sufficed for all (Bukhari).

68. Once the Holy Prophet (p.b.u.h.) had nothing to eat. He was growing weak. Hazrat Abu Talha (r.a.) went home and sent to the Prophet (p.b.u.h.) a few loaves he had in his home. The Apostle was then sitting in his Mosque in the midst of his companions. With the loaves and the companions, the Apostle arrived at the house of Talha and broke the loaves into pieces. He then asked some butter to be poured over the pieces. Thereafter he distributed the pieces among the companions. All of them ate the bread to their fill.

69. ***Hazrat Jabir (r.a.) reports:***

'My father died with a debt left behind him. It was so much that it could not be repaid with yearly crop for years. The debtors pressed for repayment. I appeared before the Apostle who went to the debtors and requested them not to press for repayment and give him some more time. But they did not agree. Thereupon the Apostle went round my garden's meagre crop and prayed to Allah. He then asked all the debtors to take back according to their claims. They took away their right but the quantity of crop remained unchanged.

70. Once, three of the Ahl-i-Suffa were alloted to Hazrat Abu Bakr (r.a.) to be fed. While they were waiting for food at his house, Abu Bakr himself was delayed with the Prophet (p.b.u.h.). When he returned home, he felt sorry for the state of affairs. Hurriedly he served the food which kept on increasing. A lot of food remained untouched, which Abu Bakr sent to the Prophet (p.b.u.h.) and a number of guests fed on it.

71. Hazrat Umme Malik (r.a.) used to send a particular bowlful of butter to the Holy Prophet (p.b.u.h.). And whenever she needed it for her children she would find enough butter left in the bowl.

One day, she wiped the bowl clean. When she went to the Apostle, he told her that had she not cleaned the bowl, she could take butter from it whenever she wanted.

72. A person was given some oats by the Holy Prophet (p.b.u.h.). Every time, he would take oats out according to his need, the stock remained as it was. One day, he weighed the remaining oats and it was finished.

The Holy Prophet (p.b.u.h.) when informed told him that if he had not weighed the oats, it would have been sufficient for his family needs.

73. During the Battle of Tabuk, there was extreme shortage of food, so much so that even the mounts were ordered to be slaughtered.

The Holy Prophet (p.b.u.h.) asked his companions to bring whatever food was left with them. Then he chanted something over it, and asked the people to take from it as much as they wanted. All of them filled their vessels with the food, but the food was still left there.

74. Once the mother of Hazrat Anas (r.a.) prepared a special dish and had a desire to serve it to the Messenger of Allah. The dish could suffice barely three persons. On being invited, the Apostle arrived with forty persons. With the prayer of the Prophet (p.b.u.h.) all the guests ate to the fill from the dish but the dish remained unfinished.

75. On Prophet's marriage with Hazrat Zainab (r.a.), Umme Saleem (r.a.) prepared a special dish and sent it to the Apostle's house.

It was meant for a few persons, but the Holy Prophet (p.b.u.h.) invited about three hundred persons. They ate it in tens at a time and the food remained unfinished.

76. Hazrat Abu Hurairah (r.a.) was once extremely hungry. When his hunger became unbearable, he sat down by the wayside. When the Prophet (p.b.u.h.) passed that way, he called him to his house. There he asked for the bowl of milk sent by someone. He sent for the Ashab-i-Suffa also. Then he asked each of them, including Abu Hurairah, to drink the milk according to their capacity. All of them took from the bowl to his fill, but the bowl remained filled to the brim.

77. Once Hazrat Miqdad (r.a.) and two of his friends became the guests of the Holy Prophet (p.b.u.h.). The guests were given three goats to be milked and the milk to be taken. The guests would drink milk and preserve the share of the Prophet (p.b.u.h.).

One night the Apostle made late. Miqdad and his friends thought that the Apostle would come back from the houses of his Companions after eating something. Hence they did not keep the share of the Apostle. But soon Miqdad rose to slaughter a goat for him. As he went to goats, he found them filled with milk. Now he started milking them. He offered the milk to the Apostle, who drank it.

78. At the time of the death of the Holy Prophet (p.b.u.h.), there was only one measure of oats left in the house of Hadrat A-'isha (R.D.) where he was lying. The measure remained full for days together until it was weighed. With the weighing, "blessing" was withdrawn.

79. Hazrat Abu Hurairah (r.a.) used to say that the loss of the tiffin-carrier was a great calamity for him. When enquired, he explained, "During a battle there was acute shortage of food. When I offered a few dates left with me, the Holy Prophet (p.b.u.h.) prayed over each

of them, mixed them up and asked the people to take their share. Those few dates sufficed the entire army and some of them were still left over. I requested the Apostle to bless the remaining dates.

Thereafter, I continued taking a few dates from the vessel according to my need. This exercise went on undisturbed till the Caliphate of Hazrat Umar (r.a.). But I lost this carrier at the disturbances caused at the martyrdom of Hazrat Usman (r.a.).

80. Once the Holy Prophet (p.b.u.h.) was visited by four hundred and fourteen persons. The Apostle asked Hazrat Umar (r.a.) to entertain them. But the later declined on the plea that he had nothing to feed them on. But on the insistence of the Apostle, he led them home and served whatever dates he had with him. Later he wondered that some dates were left even after the guests were satiated.

NEWS OF THE UNKNOWN

81. The Holy Prophet (p.b.u.h.) informed his companion about the death of Negus (Najashi) in Abyssinia. He also led the prayers for the dead king in absentia in Madina.

82. At the time of the Battle of Mota in 8 A.H., the Holy Prophet (p.b.u.h.) appointed Hazrat Zaid bin Haritha (r.a.) commander of the Muslim Army. Before the march of the army, he had prophesied that after the martydom of the commander, Ja'far shall be the commander and after him Abdullah bin Rawahah will take over and after his departure, the army will select its commander.

When the battle was going on, the Messenger of Allah was monitoring his Companions what was happening in the battlefield. He had tears in his eyes when he was narrating the tragedies. But nothing happened against what he had foretold. Khalid bin Walid was selected as new commander and victory was gained at the end.

83. In a battle a person was seen fighting very bravely. The people praised his bravery before the Prophet (p.b.u.h.). But he said that the person was a 'jahannami' (belonging to Hell). Later on, the people saw that during the fighting he received an wound which hurt him so much that he committed suicide. The prediction of the Apostle came true.

84. One person was killed in the battle fighting on the part of the Muslims. The people declared him a "jannati" (belonging to Heaven). But the Holy Prophet (p.b.u.h.) predicted against what they had said. He said that it was not possible for him to enter paradise because

during Mir-aj he had seen him in the Hell for having stolen a dress from material obtained in booty.

85. Once Umar bin Wahaab conspired with Safwaan to kill the Prophet (p.b.u.h.). He dipped his sword in poison and left for Madina. When he was passing through the streets he came across Hazrat Umar (r.a.), who caught him and produced before the Messenger of Allah.

The Apostle disclosed that he had come, in collusion with Safwaan, to kill him (the Prophet). The man got very much surprised as only Safwaan had knowledge about the plan. Thereupon, he confirmed the Prophethood of Muhammad (p.b.u.h.) and embraced Islam on the spot.

86. Once Hazrat Wabasaah (r.a.) appeared before the Holy Prophet (p.b.u.h.) with the intention to request the Apostle to explain what is good and what is evil. As he approached the Apostle, he disclosed the desire of the visitor to his wonder. Later on, the Prophet of Islam explained that 'good' is what gives 'pleasure at heart'; and 'evil' leaves the doer 'sad' or doubtful at heart.'

87. When the Holy Prophet (p.b.u.h.) arrived at Madina, a learned Jew, Abdullah bin Salaam met him and asked him three questions and the Apostle replied as under:

(1) The first sign of the approach of 'Qayamat' (Doomsday) is that there shall rage a fire which will drive people to the west from the east;

(2) the first food for the "Jannaties" (men belonging to Heaven) shall be the liver of fish.

(3) a child resembles the father when father's seed is the stronger, and it favours the mother, when mother's seed is the stronger.

Abdullah heard the answers and acknowledged the Prophethood of Muhammad (p.b.u.h.).

88. On another occasion, a learned Jew put three questions to the Holy Prophet (p.b.u.h.) for answers because only a Prophet could do it. As the Apostle answered those questions correctly and to the satisfaction of the Jew, he too acknowledged him as a true Prophet.

89. Once a few Jews asked the Prophet (p.b.u.h.) four questions with the promise that if answers to these questions were made correctly, they would embrace Islam. The Apostle answered three questions correctly as they themselves admitted. While answering the fourth one, the Messenger of Allāh said that his friend and protector among the angels was Jibrail (Gabriel) and that Jibrail was also the friend and protector of all the Prophets. Thereupon they said that they could not go along with the Prophet as Jibrail was their enemy.

90. Some of the Jews met the Holy Prophet (p.b.u.h.) and asked about the ten Commandments given to Musa (Moses). When the Apostle answered the question correctly, the Jews were so overwhelmed with joy that they kissed his hands and feet, and acknowledged him as a Prophet. Therupon the Apostle asked why did they not accept Islam, they said that they were afraid of being killed on accepting Islam.

91. On another occasion, the Holy Prophet (p.b.u.h.) was asked about "Rooh" (Soul). He kept silent. His Companions were satisfied that the Apostle would answer the question on receiving the 'Wahi' (Revelation). After sometime the Apostle, answering the question said, "Say that the soul is a thing from my Lord and that you have been given but small portion of knowledge." (Bani Israel).

92. During the Battle of Trenches, while digging the trench, a hard rock was causing great difficulty for it could not be broken by the pick. When the Holy Prophet (p.b.u.h.) was informed, he dropped down into the trench and gave such a blow with the pick that one-third of

the rock was hewed asunder. Thereupon the Apostle said, "Glory be to Allah, the keys of Syria have been given to me."

With the second blow of the pick, the Apostle hewed another one-third of the rock and said, "Glory be to Allah, the keys of Persia have been given to me. By God, I see the white castle of Madain (Ctesiphon)."

In the third attempt, the remaining portion of the rock was broken to pieces. the Apostle then said, "Glory be to Allah, I have been given the keys of Yemen. By God, I can now see the gate of San'a. (Ibn Kathir vol. III, p.194).

93. While digging the trench, whenever any party felt a difficulty owing to the existence of any hard rock which could not be broken or removed by them, the Holy Prophet (p.b.u.h.) called for some water and put a little of his saliva into it; then he prayed as Allah willed him to pray; and directed to sprinkle the water on the rock which pulverized like a heap of sand. (Ibn Hisham vol. II,-pp.217.18).

94. During the Battle of Trenches, a violent hurricane from the desert uprooted the tents of the enemies of Islam and overthrew their cooking pots. The severe weather, sent by Allah, disheartened the enemy. Calling his men, Abu Sufyan said to them, "O Quraish, it is no longer a fit place to camp here. Our horses have died, Bani Qurayza have not kept faith with us and we have heard dreadful tidings of them. You can see the havoc caused by the gale; we have neither a cooking pot at its place, nor can lit a fire, nor have tent standing, nor yet a shelter to bank on. Get you gone, for I have decided to go.

This was a miracle worked by the mercy of Allah.

95. During the Battle of Trenches, when the Mak'kan army left in embarrassment, the Holy Prophet (p.b.u.h.) said to Companions:

"The Quraish shall not come at you after this year, but you would attack them after that." (Ibn Kathir vol. III,p. 2210.

96. The terms of agreement of Hudaibia and the obligation to return without performing "Umra' plunged the Muslims into the most profound depression. It seemed incredible to them how the Messenger of Allah had agreed to those seemingly ignominious terms. So dismayed were they that Hazrat 'Umar (r.a.) went as far as to speak his mind.

The Apostle then broke camp to return to Madina. He was still in the way when Allah confirmed that the truce of Hudaibia was not a set-back but a signal victory.

Hazrat Umar (r.a.) asked the Prophet (p.b.u.h.), 'Is it a victory, O Apostle of Allah?" The Apostle replied "Yes."

The events that followed proved that the truce of Hudaibia was a decisive step in gaining victory after victory for Islam.

97. After the Treaty of Hudaibia, the Holy Prophet (p.b.u.h.) bought peace and order and started his missionary activities. The Apostle then sent several letters to the sovereigns outside Arabia and the tribal chiefs within the country inviting them to accept Islam.

When the letter of the Prophet (p.b.u.h.) was handed over to Chosroes II of Iran, he was indignant enough to tear the letter into pieces, saying, "My slave dares to write me thus!"

When his reply was conveyed to the Prophet (p.b.u.h.) he remarked, "Even so shall Allah shatter his kingdom to pieces" (Tabari vol.III, pp.90-91).

98. Chosroes II wrote to Badhan, who was his governor in Yemen, to get the Prophet of Islam sent to him in Ctesiphon. Badhan deputed Babwayh to tell the Apostle what Chosroes II had written to him and that he had come to take him to the King.

But when Babwayh came to Madina, the Apostle told him, "Allah has given Sherveh power over his father and he has killed Chosroes II. The prophecy of the Apostle came true exactly in the way foretold by him.

99. After his return from Hudaibia the Holy Prophet (p.b.u.h.) stayed in Madina for sometimes and then marched off to Khaybar. He passed the night there and ordered to march ahead before the call for prayer was given. The Muslim met the workers of Khaybar coming out with spades and baskets. As soon as they saw the Apostle and the army, they turned on their heels, shouting, 'Muhammad and his force."

The Apostle said, "Allah is Great. Khaybar is destroyed." (Ibn Hisham vol.III, pp.229-30).

100. The slave of a Jew of Khaybar had been hired to watch over the flocks of his master. When he saw the Jews taking up arms for giving a fight to the Muslims, he asked, "What for do you go?" The Jews replied that they were going to fight the man who had laid a claim to prophethood. The slave's curiosity brought him to the Prophet (p.b.u.h.) whom he asked about the faith preached by him. The Apostle replied, 'I call you to Islam, that is, you bear witness that there is no deity save Allah and that I am the Apostle of Allah, and you serve not aught except Allah."

"If I bear witness as you say," enquired the slave, "and have faith in Allah, what shall I get in return?"

The Apostle replied, "If you die with Faith, you will enter Paradise."

The slave accepted Islam and then asked the Apostle, "What should I do with the flock? I hold it in trust."

The Apostle told him to abandon the goats in the field near the fort and Allah would cause them to reach their owner. The man did so and the goats did find their way back to their master.

101. During the Battle of Khaybar, a Bedouin came to the Apostle and after accepting Islam expressed his desire to accompany him in the expedition. The Apostle asked some of his Companions to take care of him and see his needs. When the Muslims captured one of the forts and won a large booty, the men had taken out a herd of cattle for grazing. The spoil was distributed among the combatants and the share of the Bedouin was also apportioned. When he was given his share, he took it to the Apostle and asked, "What is it?" The Apostle explained that it was his share of the booty of war. Thereupon he said, "I didn't come to you for it." Then pointing to his throat he continued, "I followed you in the hope that I would be hit by an arrow here and would go to paradise." The Apostle replied, "If you desire it so, Allah will do likewise."

Then, in a subsequent battle at Khaybar the dead body of the Bedouin was found among those killed in encounter. The Apostle asked, "Is it the same man?" When the Companions replied in the affirmative, the Apostle remarked, "He was true to Allah and Allah made his wish come true."

102. Hazrat Amr bin Salim al-Khuza (r.a.) went to the Apostle in Madina and recited verses describing how the Quraish had violated their pledged word. He asked the Apostle to extend his help by virtue of the treaty of alliance between him and the Khuza'a.

We took the stand that the Quraish had annulled the treaty with the Prophet (p.b.u.h.) by attacking his allies when they were at their well and had not spared their lives even when they were performing prayers. After listening to his complaint the Prophet (p.b.u.h.) replied:

"You will be helped, O 'Amr bin Salim."

The Prophet (p.b.u.h.) then sent a man to Mak'kah in order to get a confirmation of the affair and also to allow the Quraish to redress the wrong committed by them.

The Apostle directed to place three alternatives before the Quraish;

a) they should either pay the blood money for the victims of Khuza'a;

b) or terminate their alliance with the aggressors belonging to Bani Nifasa of Banu Bakr; but

c) falling these they shall get in return what they had alone. The terms were communicated to the Quraish but in the fit of their pride they replied:

"Yes, we would prefer measure for measure."

The Muslims were thus absolved of their undertaking with the Quraish and it became incumbent on them to get satisfaction of the wrong done to their allies.

When the Prophet (p.b.u.h.) was informed of the reply given by Quraish, he said;

"I see if Abu Sufyan has come to you to strengthen the treaty and to ask for more time."

The events took shape as predicted by the Apostle. The Quraish realised the gravity of the situation and felt sorry for the indiscreet reply given by the thoughtless among them. They charged Abu Sufyan to get the treaty ratified and extended again. (Zad al-Ma'ad vol.1, p.120).

103. When the Holy Prophet (p.b.u.h.) decided to proceed for the conquest of Mak'kah, he asked the Muslims to start making preparations for an expedition but also bade them to keep it a secret. Later on, the Apostle informed the men that he intended to go to Mak'kah and ordered them to get ready for it. He also prayed.

"O Allah! confound the spies and the informers of the Quraish so that we may take them by surprise in their land." (Zaad-al-Ma'ad Vol.I,p.421)

Hatib bin Abi Balta'a was one of those Muhajireen who had migrated from Mak'kah and had taken part in the Battle of Badr. It is related that when the Holy Prophet (p.b.u.h.) informed his companions about his intention to attack Mak'kah and they quietly started making preparations for it, Hatib bin Abi Balta'a wrote a letter to the Quraish about the intended attack and gave it to a woman for delivering it to the Quraish. Hatib also promised to give some money to the woman who set off for Mak'kah after putting the letter in her head and plaiting her locks over it. The voice of Heaven informed the Apostle about the action of Hatib. He immediately sent Hazrat Ali (r.a.) and Hazrat Zubayr (r.a.) in her pursuit, saying:

"Go until you come to the meadow of Khaakh, where you will find a woman travelling on a camel who has a letter which you must take from her."

The two went off racing on their horses until they came to the meadow, and there they found the woman going on her camel. They made her dismount and searched her baggage but found nothing. At last Hazrat Ali (r.a.) said to her:

"By Allah, the Messenger of Allah is not mistaken nor are we. You must bring out the letter or we will search your person."

When she saw that they were in earnest, she asked them to turn aside. Then she drew out the letter from her tresses and handed it over to them. The letter, brought back to Apostle, had been written by Hatib bin Abi Batla'a informing the Quraish about the departure of the Muslim army. When summoned by the Apostle, Hatib bin Balta'a said:

"O Messenger of Allah, don't be hasty with me. I swear to Allah that I have faith in Allah and His Apostle; neither I have abandoned nor changed my faith. I had been attached as an ally to the Quraish and was not one of them; I have my family there but no kinsmen to protect them. Other emigrants with you have their relations among the Quraish who will take care of their families. I thought that as I did not have that advantage I should give them some help so that they might protect my relations."

Hazrat 'Umar bin Khattab (r.a.) sought permission of the Holy Prophet (p.b.u.h) to cut off Hatib's head whom he charged as being a hypocrite, disloyal to Allah and His Messenger. But the Apostle replied:

"He was present at Badr. Do you know, 'Umar', perhaps Allah has looked favourably on those who were present at Badr."

"Do as you wish for I have forgiven you."

Umar (r.a.) dissolved into tears, saying:

"Allah and His Messenger know better."

The Apostle set out from Madina, during Ramadhan, at the head of ten thousand companions. The army made camp at Marr al-Zahraan. The Quraish were, however, still uncertain, for Allah had kept them completely ignorant of the advance of the Muslim army.

104. After the Conquest of Mak'kah the Holy Prophet (p.b.u.h.) first cleared the Ka'ba of three hundred and sixty idols after the return of normalcy.

Thereafter the Holy Prophet (p.b.u.h.) went round the sancturary. Then he sent for Uthman bin Talha, who had the charge of the Ka'aba's keys. He took the keys from 'Uthman and got the doors opened.

Once, before his migration to Madina, the Apostle had requested 'Uthman' to give him the keys of the Ka'aba, but Uthman had not only refused his request but had also been impertinent to him. With exemplary forbearance the Apostle had then said to him;

"Uthman, the day will come when you will see this key in my hands. I would then give it to whom I would like."

"If the day comes, the Quraish would be humiliated and crushed that day."

"No, the Prophet (p.b.u.h.) had said calmly,

"It would be the day when they would be honoured and secured."

It is related that the prediction had so haunted the mind of 'Uthman that he had come to believe that it would happen exactly as foretold by the Apostle. (Zaad-al-Ma'aad vol.I, p.425, Bukhari).

105. Fadala bin 'Umayr wanted to kill the Holy Prophet (p.b.u.h.). He made up his mind to attack the Apostle when he would be busy in circumambulating the Ka'ba. When he drew near, the Apostle called out:

"Fadala" to invite his attention.

He replied, “Yes, O Apostle of Allah.”

The Apostle then asked him:

“What are you thinking about?”

"Nothing" replied Fadala, “I was recollecting Allah.”

The Apostle smiled and said:

“Seek forgiveness from Allah,” and at the same time he put his hand on Fadala’s chest. His heart was atonce set at ease and, as Fadala related later on:

“The Holy Prophet (p.b.u.h.) had not yet removed his hand from my chest that I found him dearer to my heart than every creature of Allah.”

Fadala further says:

“Then I went back to my house and passed the woman with whom I used to converse. She asked me to sit down and talk with her, but I replied, “No, Allah and Islam do not permit it now.” (Ibn Hisham vol.II, p.417).

106. The people of Mak’kah who had joined the Holy Prophet (p.b.u.h.) in this battle were fresh from paganism. Now, in the days of pagan past, some tribes of Arabia used to venerate a great green tree known as Dhat-u-Anwaat under which they stayed for a day, suspended their weapon to its branches and offered sacrifices beneath it. When these men were going with the army they happened to pass by a big shady tree which reminded them of the past fetishism. They immediately requested the Apostle:

“Make us a tree as they used to have Dhat-u-Anwaat, O Messenger of Allah.”

The Prophet (p.b.u.h.) replied:

"Allah is great! By Him who holds my life in His hands, you say what the people of Mu-sa (Moses) said to him: Make for us a God even as they have gods. He (Musa) said: Lo! you are a folk who know not." (Q.7:138).

The Apostle then added:

"Verily, you would follow every custom of the people before you." (Ibn Hisham, vol. II, p.442).

107. It was the 10th of Shawwal, 8 A.H., when the Muslim army reached Hunayn, descending the 'wadi' (valley) in morning twilight. The enemy had already taken its position in the glens and hollows and craters of the valley. A valley of arrows was all that the Muslims saw of the enemy, then suddenly the enemy followed up the attack with full force. Hawaazin were celebrated archers.

The sudden onslaught forced the Muslim flanks to fall back and they fled in terror none heeding the other. The battle had taken a dangerous turn; a complete rout of the Muslims was in sight without any possibility of an orderly retreat or rallying of their forces again. Like the Uhad, when the rumour of the Apostle's death had disheartened the Muslims, the troops were once more driven to despair in Hunayn by a similar misgiving.

Some of the rude fellows from Mak'kah who had joined the Muslim army but were still not strong in faith started talking in a way that let out their antipathy to Islam. One said:

"There flight will not stop before they get at the sea."

"Another man remarked:

"The spell of their sorcery has ended today.

The Muslim had to suffer this defeat after the brilliant victory of Mak'kah as if by way of punishment for their reliance on numbers instead of the succour of Allah. Their faith needed to be strengthened by a misadventure for they had to learn the lesson that both victory and defeat came from Allah; neither the one should make man exultant nor the other despondent. The Muslims were all over with their trepidation when the peace of Allah appeared to be descending on them and the Apostle. The Prophet (p.b.u.h.) had all the while stood firm on his place, riding his white mule, without any fear. Only a few of the Ansar and Muhajirin or his relatives were then with him. Abbas bin Abdul Muttalib was holding the bridle of his mule while the Apostle of Allah was calling aloud:

"Verify, I am the Prophet without falsehood; I am son of Abdul Muttalib." (According to Bukhari Abu Sufyan bin Harith was holding the bridle).

In the meantime a detachment of the enemy advanced towards him. The Apostle took a handful of dust and threw it into their eyes.

When the Holy Prophet (p.b.u.h.) saw his men in confusion, he said

"O Abbas call out, O Ansar, O comrades of the ocacia tree."

All those who heard the cry, respondend:

"Here are we."

Abbas had a loud voice. Whoever heard him calling got off from his camel and came to the Holy Prophet (p.b.u.h.).

When sufficient number of men had gathered, they bore down upon the enemy. A combat between the two parties started afresh. The Apostle then took to a height alongwith some of his comapnaions. He saw the two sides grappled with one another. He said:

"Now the battle has grown hot."

He threw a few pebbles on the enemy. Abbas relates:

"I saw the enemy becoming slack thereafter and losing the day to the Muslims."

Both the armies fought bravely. However, before all those Muslims who had fled away had come back, the enemy was discomfited and a party of handcuffed prisoners was brought before the Holy Prophet (p.b.u.h.). Allah helped the Apostle with the hosts of heaven to win the day and brought Hawaazin to their knees.

The Holy Qur'an narrates it as under:

"Allah has given you victory on many fields and on the day of Hunayn, when you exulted in your multitude but it availed you naught, and the earth, vast as is, was straightened for you; then you turned back in flight;

Then Allah sent His peace of assurance down upon His Messenger and upon the believers, and punished those who disbelieved. Such is the reward of Disbelievers." (Q. 9.25-26).

108. After distributing the spoils and captives of the Battle of Taif at Jirrana, the Apostle put on the "Ihram" for performing 'Umra' for this was the place from where the people going for pilgrimage to Mak'kah from Taif changed into "Ihram". Having completed the lesser pilgrimage the Apostle returned to Madina.

The Apostle came back to Madina in Dhi Q'ada, 8 A.H. While the forces were returning from Taif, the Apostle of Allah asked the men to recite:

"We are those who revert and repent and worship and glorify our Lord."

Some of the people then asked the Holy Prophet (p.b.u.h.) to call down evil on Thaqif.

The Apostle raised his hands to entreat:

"O Allah! Guide Thaqif on the right path and bring them here."

Urwa bin Mas'ud al Thaqafi met the Apostle while he was on his way back to Madina. He became a Muslim and returned to his people for inviting them to Islam. He was very popular and enjoyed the esteem of his clansmen but when he broke the news that he had accepted Islam, the people turned against him. They shot arrows at him from all directions; one hit him and he died.

The Thaqif held out for a few months after killing Urwa but after taking counsel among them they reached the conclusion that it would be beyond their power to fight all those tribes which had already taken the oath of allegiance at the hands of the Apostle. Ultimately, they decided to send a deputation to the Apostle.

When the deputation of Thaqif came to Madina, a tent was pitched for them in the Prophets's Mosque. They requested the Apostle not to destroy their chief deity, the idol of al-Laat, for three years. The Apostle refused; then they continued to reduce the period by one year, but the Apostle remained firm in refusing their request until they finally asked for a period of one month after they had returned to their homes. The Apostle again rejected their request and ordered Abu Sufyan and Mughira bin Sh'uba al-Thaqafi to destroy al-Laat. Thereafter the Thaqif asked the Prophet (p.b.u.h.) that they might be excused from offering prayers. To this the Apostle replied:

"Nothing remains of a religion which has no prayer."

Abu Sufyan and Mughira bin Sh'uba accompanied the deputation of Thaqif when they returned to Taif. Mughira smote al-

Laat with a pickaxe and broke it into pieces. Thereupon the people of Taif accepted Islam; not one of them remained attached to paganism. (Zaad-al-Ma'ad vol.I, pp. 458-59).

109. Spread of Islam among the tribes further aggravated the resentment of the Quraish. They came together and decided to draw up a decree ostracising Bani Hashim and Bani Abdul Muttalib.

1. It was decided that nobody should marry the women of these two clans nor give their women to them in marriage;

2. Neither anybody should buy from them nor sell to them.

Having solemnly agreed to these points, the agreement was put into writing and parchment was hung in the K'aba in order to give it a religious sanction thereby making it mandatory for all.

Bani Hashim and Bani Abdul Muttalib joined Abu Talib after the boycott was enforced and withdrew to a narrow glen or 'wadi' known as Sh'eb Abi Talib. It was the seventh year of the Prophet's mission.

Weeks and months passed, and the people of Hashim lived in misery and hunger. The ban was so rigorously imposed that the Prophet's clan was reduced to eating leaves of acacia and the cries of hungry children echoed all over the valley. The caravans passed peacefully through the streets of Mak'kah but the Quraish told the merchants not to buy or sell anything to the forsaken clans with the result that they pegged the prices so high that it was well nigh impossible for the beleaguered people to purchase even the bare necessities.

The decree of proscription lasted for three years — for three years Bani Hashim and Bani Abdul Muttalib lived in exile and endured the hardships of blockade.

But all the people of the Quraish were not utterly deprived. Those among them who were well-natured and kind-hearted occasionally supplied food secretly to the exiles. However, the Apostle never ceased preaching the message he had brought to his own people, and, even to others, whenever he got the opportunity. Bani Hashim on their part, endured every trouble with exemplary patience and fortitude.

The pitiable condition of the exiles gave rise to a feelings of indignation against the ban among the gracious and genial sons of the desert. Hisham bin 'Amr bin Rabi'a took the initiative to end the boycott. He was amiable and kind-hearted as well as highly esteemed by the Quraish. He contacted some other considerate and well-disposed persons and put them to shame for allowing the tyranny to linger on.

At last, Hisham supported by four other persons agreed to stand together till the decree of boycott was cancelled. On the morrow, when the Quraish had assembled in the sanctuary, Zuhayr whose mother 'Atika was daughter of Abdul Muttalib, cried out to the people;

"O ye people of Mak'kah, shall we eat and drink while Bani Hashim should die of hunger, unable even to buy or sell? By Allah I will not take rest until this cruel and unjust decree is torn to pieces."

Abu Talib was also sitting in the corner of Ka'aba. He disclosed that Muhammad had already told him that Allah has given white ants power over the document. He also declared that had that not come true he would give up support to Muhammad. This disclosure made the matter very interesting and sensational. All those assembled there waited to know the truth.

When, inspite of intervention from Abu Jah'l, Mut'im bin Adiy went up to tear the document into pieces, he found that with the exception of the words "In Thy name, O Allah" the rest of the document had already been eaten up by white ants.

The blighted document was, however, taken out and thrown away and thus ended the boycott and what was written on it. (Ibn Hisham vol.1,pp.350-51).

110. The number of the Prophet's followers increased day by day threatening to turn the tide against Quraish; they felt the situation highly embarrassing but were unable to do anything to stem the tide of Islam.

Utba bin Rabi'a the old and wise patrician of the Quraish realised that he must find a way to patch up the differences with the Apostle. He consulted the Quraish to make some concessions to the Apostle so that he might give up his mission. The Quraish thought it to be workable proposition and allowed him to negotiate with the Prophet on their behalf.

'Utba went to the Apostle and sat by his side. Then he said:

"O my nephew, you know the worthy position you enjoy among us. But you have created a rift in your people by ridiculing them, insulting their gods as well as their religion, declaring their forefathers as heathens and denying their customs. Now, listen to me, I will make some suggestions, happly you may find one of these acceptable."

The Holy Prophet (p.b.u.h.) replied,

"O Abul Walid, go on, I am listening."

'Utba continued;

"My nephew, if you want to have wealth by what you preach, we will collect enough of it that you will be the richest of us; if you desire honour, we will make you our chief and leave every decision to your choice; if you aspire for kingship, we will recognize you as our monarch; and if you are possessed of a ghost or a jinn of which you have no remedy, we will find a skilful physician for you and spend our wealth lavishly until your health is completely restored."

The Apostle listened patiently. When 'Utba had finished, he asked,

"Is it all that you have to say?"

"Yes", replied 'Utba.

"Now listen to me", said the Prophet (p.b.u.h.):

"In the name of Allah, the Compassionate, the Merciful ...

and he cōntinued to recite the Sura Fussilat,

ending the recitation at prostration."

When 'Utba heard the revelation, he listened with rapt attention, putting his hands behind him and leaning on them. The recitation ended, the Prophet (p.b.u.h.) prostrated and then said to Utba:

"Abul Walid, you have heard what you have heard,

now it is for you to decide."

As the Quraish saw Utba returning, they said:

"Honest to God, he comes with an altered expression of his face."

And when he came near they asked him what had happened.

"I have heard a discourse the like of which I had never heard before. I'II swear to God, O Quraish, that it is neither poetry, nor spells, nor witchcraft. Take my advice and let this man alone."

The Quraish reviled 'Utba, and said:

"You have been bewitched by his tongue."

"This is my opinion," replied Utba, "Now you may do whatever you think fit." (Ibn Hisham, vol.I,pp. 293-94).

111. The Quraish offered a reward of one hundred camels to anyone who brought back the Apostle, dead or alive, while he was on his way to Madina. On the other hand, the Apostle spent three nights in the cave and then guided by Amir bin Fuhayrah went along the road by the seacoast.

Suraqa bin Malik bin Ju'shum heard of the price set by the Quraish on the head of the Apostle and hurried after him. The reward of a hundred camels was too much for him; he got up on his mare and went after the fugitives tracking their footsteps. He let his mare go in a canter until he nearly overtook the fugitives. But his mare stumbled abruptly, and he was thrown off. He rose, got hold of his quiver, and remounted the mare, and let her go ahead. His mare again stumbled and he was again thrown off, but he continued the chase until he could see the three men going ahead. Suddenly, his mare stumbled for the third time, its fore-legs sinking up to the knees in the ground, and he was thrown off again. He also saw dust rising from the ground like a sandstorm.

Suraqa was now convinced that the Apostle was protected against him and he would not in any case triumph over him. He called but saying that he was Suraqa bin Ju'shum and that no harm would come to them from him. The Apostle asked Abu Bakr:

"Ask him what he wants from us?"

"Suraqa answered:

"Write for me a warrant of security."

Thereupon the Holy Prophet (p.b.u.h.) ordered Amir bin

Fuhayrah to write the warrant which he wrote on a piece of tanned leather or bone. Suraqa preserved the writing for long as a memorial.

112. While migrating to Madina, Hazrat Abu Bakr and the Holy Prophet (p.b.u.h.) passed by the tent of Umm M'abad, a woman of Khuza'a, who had a milch ewe but its udder had dried up owing to draught.

Allah's Messenger wiped its udder with his hand and mentioning the name of Almighty Allah, he prayed that Umm M'abad might have a blessing in her ewe. It then gave a flow of milk. He first gave Umm M'abad and others a drink until all of them were fully satisfied; he drank himself last of all.

He milked it a second time, and when the vessel was full he left it with her.

When Abu M'abad came back and his wife told him about the prodigious happening and the angelic stranger, he replied:

"By Allah, he appears to be the same man of the Quraish whom they are prowling after."

112. After the death of Abdul Muttalib, Abu Talib took the Apostle under his care for he and Abdullah, the Apostle's father, were brothers by the same mother. Abdul Muttalib had also been insisting upon Abu Talib to take care of the Apostle. Accordingly, Abu Talib took the Apostle under his protection and treated him with more care and affection than his own sons, Ali, Ja'far and Aqil.

Once, when the Apostle was nine years old, Abu Talib planned to go in a merchant caravan to Syria. The Apostle approched his uncle, and nestling close to him, insisted on accompanying him in the journey. Abu Talib felt moved and agreed to take him to Syria.

When the caravan reached Busra in Syria, it broke the journey for a short stay, where lived a monk, Buhaira by name, in his cell. He came out, against his practice, to welcome the merchants and made a great feast for them. The caravan found favour with Buhaira, so they relate, because of something he had seen while in his cell. When Buhaira saw the Apostle of Allah, he satisfied himself of the signs of apostleship he had known, and advised Abu Talib:

"Return to your home with this youth, and guard him from the Jews; for great dignity awaits your nephew."

Abu Talib took the Apostle off quickly to Mak'kah as advised by Buhaira.

113. ***Opening of The Chest:***

In accordance with the Arabian custom, in order to learn the pure Arabic dilect (and to enjoy the pleasant atmosphere of the countryside at the same time) the baby (Muhammad p.b.u.h.) was given in the custody of the nurse Halimah, who visited Mak'kah during those days in search of a rich baby to bring up but was not successful; hence was obliged to accept orphan (Muhammad p.b.u.h.) as it was heavenly destined for her.

In all, baby Muhammad (p.b.u.h.) spent six years with her among the Banu Sa'd, during that time he developed the purest dialect of Arabic about which he spoke later:

"Verily, I am the most eloquent Arab amongst you;

my descendant is from the Quraish and I speak the tongue of Banu Sa'd."

Once when Muhammad (p.b.u.h.) was playing with children, two angels in snow-white dress came down from the heaven and opened his holy chest. They took out some black pieces of flesh from it. Then they washed the heart and inner side of the chest from the "snow water" they brought with them in a gold dish from the Heaven.

It is also narrated that they also fixed the "Seal" of the Prophets at the same time in between the two shoulders on the back and then went back.

Seeing all this, his foster-brother and other boys with whom he was playing were frightened and ran to Lady Halimah, but when she reached there the angels had left.

However, Muhammad (p.b.u.h.) told her all the story and said that they filled a kind of divine light but he was not hurt at all.

114. In those days reading and writing was not in vogue in Arabia and the business minded Quraish regarded it a task for menials, therefore he was not educated. Afterwards this unlettered orphan became the repository of the highest wisdom. Though himself untaught by a worldly teacher, he became the teacher of mankind which was one of his Great Miracles.

The Holy Qur'an speaks about it:

"Those who follow the Apostle, the unlettered Prophet, whom they find mentioned in Torah (Old Testament). He commands them what is just and good, and forbids them what is evil; he allows them as lawful what is good (and pure) and prohibits them from what is bad (and impure). He releases them from their heavy burdens and from the yokes that are upon them. So it is those who believe in him, honour him; help him, and follow the Light which is sent down with him — it is they who will prosper."

"Say: O men! I am sent unto you all, as the Apostle of Allah, to whom belongs the dominion of the heavens and the earth, there is no god but He. It is He that gives both life and death. So believe in Him and His Apostle, the unlettered Prophet, who believes in Allah and His words: follow him that you may be guided." (Q.7:157-58).

115. ***Conversion of Jinns To Islam:***

After the death of Abu Talib the oppositon of Mak'kah grew greater day by day and the enemies of Islam began to redouble their persecution. The Holy Prophet (p.b.u.h.) was then forced to turn his attention towards the next biggest city of Arabia: Taif.

He travelled to Taif and invited its inhabitants towards Islam. But all the chieftains of the clan refused even to listen to the Holy Prophet (p.b.u.h.) and treated him most contemptuously and rudely. When he was leaving the town they told a gang of vagabounds to pelt him with stones. He was so much pelted that his whole body was besmeared with blood and his shoes were clogged to his feet.

The Holy Prophet (p.b.u.h.) left the town in this woeful plight while praying to Allah:

"O Allah! To Thee I complain of the feebleness of my strength, of my lack of resourcefulness and my insignificance in the eyes of people. O 'Most Merciful of all, capable of showing mercy! Thou art the Lord of the weak and Thou art my own Lord. To whom art Thou entrust me, to an unsympathetic foe who would sullenly frown at me, or to an alien to whom Thou hast given control over my affair. Not in the least do I care for anything except that I may have Thy protection for myself. In the light of Thy face do I seek shelter — the light of which illumines the Heaven and dispels all sorts of darkness, and which controls all affairs in this world as well as in the Hereafter. May it never be that I should incur Thy wrath, or that Thou should be displeasure with me. I must remove the cause of Thy displeasure till Thou art pleased. There is no strength nor power but through Thee."

Bleeding and exhausted, the Holy Prophet (p.b.u.h.) marched onward to Mak'kah. His shoes were besmeared with blood. On his return to Mak'kah during the night, he offered Salaat at Nakhla, a place in suburbs of Mak'kah.

While he was offering Salaat, a group of Jinns passed by him. They were seven in number. The Jinns listened to the Holy Qur'-an which was being recited by the Holy Prophet (p.b.u.h.). After he completed his Salaat, they requested him to allow them to enter the folds of Islam. The Holy Qur'-an points out towards this as under:

"Say (O Muhammad!): It is revealed to me that a company of the Jinns gave ear, and they said: Lo! it is a marvellous Qur'an which guides to righteousness, so we believed in it and we shall not join (in worship) any (gods) with our Lord." (Q.72:1-2).

116. ***Divine Help:***

In the Battle of Badr, the Quraish reached the battlefield earlier and occupied the points of advantage. The Muslims could not get any well or spring. Moreover the sandy soil was causing the feet of camels to sink. Then it was suggested by Hubaab bin Mundhir (R.A.) to take possession of a nearly big spring. The suggestion was accepted by the Holy Prophet (p.b.u.h.) and he asked the Muslims to take over the spring. By the grace of Allah, it rained heavily and small reservoirs were improvised for storing water.

The Holy Qur'an speaks about this as follows:

"And He sent down water from sky that thereby He might purify you." (Q. 8:2).

117. ***Praying All The Night:***

The Holy Prophet (p.b.u.h.) prayed all the night at Badr, weeping and repeating the following words:

"O Allah, should You suffer this small band of Believers to perish this day, no one will be left on earth to worship Thee." (Ibn Hisham Book I Vols.1+2).

Allah answered the prayer and gave glad tidings of victory through the following revelation (Bukhari).

"Soon shall the enemy be routed and will then turn and flee....." (Q. 54:45).

118. ***Glorious Victory:***

The victory at the Badr was a clear help of Almighty Allah. Indeed, it was a glorious spiritual victory of the Truth ('Haq') over the Falsehood ('Batil')—with marvellous Divine Help. The Holy Qur'an speaks about this as under:

"Indeed there was a sign for you in the two Hosts which met together in encounter; one party fights in the Way of Allah, and the other unbelieving .... and Allah strengthens with His aid whom He pleases; most surely there is a lession in this for those who have eyes to see." (Q. 3:12).

119. ***The Holy Qur'an again says:***

"Allah had helped you at Badr, when you were contemptible little force; then fear Allah in order to show your gratitude." When you did say to the believers: Does it not suffice you that your Lord should help you with three thousand angels sent down." (Q. 3: 123-24).

According to the historians the angels referred in the above verse (3:124) came down with three arch angels viz. Jibrail, Micka'il and Isra'fil, each of them was accompanied by 1,000 angels.

120. ***Angelic Warriors:***

Coming down of the angelic warriors is attested by a peasant (who had not accepted Islam by then) who was attending sheep on an adjacent hill. He says:

"I was with a companion, my cousin, upon the fold of mountain watching the battle and waiting to join with the conquerors and share the spoil. Suddenly we beheld a great cloud sailing towards us, and within it were the neighing of steeds and braying of trumpets. As it approached, squadrons of angels sallied forth, and we heard the terrific voice of archangel as he urged his more Haizum, "speed! Speed! Oh Haizum!" Due to that awful sound, the heart of my companion burst with terror, and he died on the spot, and I had well nigh shared his fate."

This miraculous aid is repeatedely mentioned in the Holy Qur'an as also quoted above.

121. ***Throwing Of Dust At The Enemy:***

When the Battle of Badr began, the Holy Prophet (p.b.u.h.) prayed, and threw a handful of dust (or sand) at enemy, symbolical of their rushing blindly to their fate. Every act in the battle is ascribed to Allah ,as it was in His cause, and it was not undertaken except by His Command. The Holy Qur'an points out towards it as under:

"It was not you who slew them, it was Allah: When you threw (a handful of dust), it was not your act, but Allah's: In order that He might test the Believers by a gracious trial from Himself: for Allah is He who hears and knows (all things)." (Q. 8:17)

122. ***Piece Of Rod Turning Into Sword:***

Ukkashah bin Mihsan, a companion, was fighting in the battle. During the fight his sword broke down. The Holy Prophet (p.b.u.h.) gave him a piece of rod which turned into a sword, as soon as he took it from Prophet's hand. He fought with that sword. He named that sword as "Al-Awn" which remained with him in all the following battles. (Ibn Hisham Book 1, vol. 1+2 p.637)

123. ***Predictions Of Peace And Plentitude:***

Once Addi bin Haatim (r.a.) was sitting with the Holy Prophet (p.b.u.h.) that two persons came along. One complained of starvation and the other of highway robberies;

"The Holy Prophet (p.b.u.h.) turned towards Addi and said:

"If he (Addi) lived till then, he would see that a veiled (purdahnasheen) woman would travel on camel back from Hira and reach the K'aba unmolested fearing none but Allah that the treasures of Iran will be conquered and that a person may walk around with fistfuls of gold and silver for distribution among the poor but none would be interested!"

Addi (r.a.) narrated that he wondered greatly at the predictions, but he lived to see the first two predictions fulfilled and he was one of those who plundered the treasures of Iran.

And the third prediction too, according to reliable tradition came true during the time of the Bani Umayyah.

124. ***Naming Of Quraish Chiefs To Be Killed At Badr:***

Before the Battle of Badr began, the Holy Prophet (p.b.u.h.) toured the battleground and pointed out to his companions the places where each of the Quraish chiefs was to fall.

After the battle the Companions found to their wonder that each and every prediction came true.

It is considerable that before the battle there was no hope for such a poorly armed army of three hundred Muslims to win the battle.

125. ***Prediction About The Death Of Hazrat Fatimah:***

During his last illness, when the Holy Prophet (p.b.u.h.) found his beloved daughter Hazrat Fatimah (r.a.), he called her near and whispered something that made her weap; but when he again whispered something she began to smile.

When Hazrat Aisha (r.a.) asked Hazrat Fatimah (r.a.) as to what the Apostle whispered in her ears, she declined to disclose the matter. But after the demise of the Holy Prophet (p.b.u.h.) when Hazrat Aisha (r.a.) insisted again, Hazrat Fatimah (r.a.) revealed that when the Apostle predicted his death she started weeping; but when she was told by the Messenger of Allah that she (Fatimah) will be the first from his family to join him, she smiled.

Both these predictions of the Holy Prophet (p.b.u.h.) were found to be correct.

126. ***Prediction Of His Own Death:***

During the last Hajj the Holy Prophet (p.b.u.h.) told the gathering that he may, perhaps, not seen there next year.

The year of his death, the Holy Prophet (p.b.u.h.) told Sa'ad bin Mua'dh (r.a.), who was proceeding on to Yemen, that he might not see him on his return.

Again, a few days before his demise, he said that Almighty Allah had given a choice between the world and the life of the Hereafter; and that he had chosen the later.

127. ***Conquest Of Countries:***

The Holy Prophet (p.b.u.h.) had predicted conquests of Syria, Yemen and Iran while digging the trench at the Battle of Trenches. These predictions came true later.

Syria was conquered by Hazrat Khalid bin Walid (r.a.) during the Caliphate of Hazrat Umar ibn Khattab (r.a.).

Yemen was conquered in 8 A.H. during the Caliphate of Hazrat Umar bin Khattab (r.a.).

Iran was conquered by Hazrat Sa'ad bin Abi Waqqas (r.a.) during the Caliphate of Hazrat Umar ibn Khattab (r.a.).

The Holy Prophet (p.b.u.h.) had predicted a high place of honour for Hazrat Sa'ad bin Abi Waqqas (r.a.) and said that many will gain by his acts and many others lose.

This was an indication of his conquest of Iran when the Muslims gained and the Magis lost.

128. The Holy Prophet (p.b.u.h.) had predicted that Egypt would soon be conquered by the Muslims. He had further said that Egyptians should be treated kindly as they were related to Arabs (Hazrat Ibrahim's wife and mother of Hazrat Ismail was from Egypt).

129. The Holy Prophet (p.b.u.h.) had predicted the fall of Bait-ul-Maqdis to Muslims. He had also predicted that it would fall after his death.

This prediction came true during the Caliphate of Hazrat Umar ibn Khattab (r.a.).

130. One day the Holy Prophet (p.b.u.h.) was in deep sleep. All of a sudden he woke up smiling and said:

"I saw some of my Ummah sitting on a royal throne and sailing the Mediterranian for Jehad."

This dream came true during the time of Amir Mu'wiyya (r.a.) when the Muslims sat on the royal throne for the first time in Damascus; and Prince Yazeed sailed to Constantinople.

131. ***Apostasy:***

The Holy Prophet (p.b.u.h.) had predicted that 'apostasy' will raise head after his final departure and a number of false prophets will rise in various parts of Arabia and be joined by some Muslims.

The prediction proved correct during the time of Caliph Hazrat Abu Bakr Siddique (r.a.).

132. ***Umme Waraqa:***

Umme Waraqa (r.a.) had requested permission to join 'Jihad' at the time of Badr. But the Holy Prophet (p.b.u.h.) had asked her to stay at home to die as a 'Shaheed' (martyr).

The prediction came true at the time of Caliph Hazrat Umar Ibn Khattab (r.a.), when a slave man and a slave girl strangled her to death. And this tragedy occured at her home and thus she got the status of 'Shaheed' as predicted by the Apostle.

133. ***Evil From The East:***

Once the Holy Prophet (p.b.u.h.) pointed his finger towards the east and predicted that evil shall come to the Muslims from this direction (Iraq falling in the east).

The prediction came true in more than one way.

The murderer of Caliph Hazrat Umar ibn Khattab (r.a.) was an 'Ajami'.

The evil during the third Caliph Hazrat Uthman bin Affan (r.a.) rose from Iraq and spread up to Egypt.

Both the Battle of Jamal and Battle of Siffin fought between fourth Caliph Hazrat Ali (r.a.) and Amir Mu'awiyyah (r.a.) took place in Iraq.

Khwarij-e-Islam rose from Iraq.

The Jabriah and Qadriah sects which shattered the unity and purity of Muslim beliefs were born there.

Karbala falls in Iraq

The evil of Mukhtar took place there.

Hajjaj bin Yusuf perpetrated his cruelties on the same soil. The depredations of the Mongols and the Turks took place there.

134. ***Prediction About A Wife:***

Once the Holy Prophet (p.b.u.h.) had predicted before his wives that one of them shall have barking dogs at her at Howaab.

When Hazrat Aisha (r.a.) joined the Battle of Jamal in Basra (Iraq) and reached the period of Howaab, the dogs started barking at her. Thus the prediction of the Apostle proved to be correct.

135. ***Imam Hasan:***

Once the Holy Prophet (p.b.u.h.) took his maternal grandson Hazrat Hasan (r.a.) with him on to the pulpit of the Prophet's Mosque and told the congregation:

"One day Hasan will bring about compromise between two groups.

Six months after the "Shahadat" (martyrdom) of the fourth Caliph of Islam Hazrat Ali (r.a.), Hasan effected a compromise between the camp followers of Hazrat Ali (r.a.) and Amir Muawiyyah (r.a.).

136. Once the Holy Prophet (p.b.u.h.) had predicted that the upstart Quraish will bring about untold miseries to Islam.

This prediction also came true because martyrdom of the third Caliph of Islam, Hazrat Uthman Ghani (r.a.), was the result of their ambition; so also the Battle of Jamal between Hazrat Ali (r.a.) and Amir Muawiyyah (r.a.) was fought because of their high ambitions once again. History bears witness to this fact. And thus the prediction made by the Apostle proved truthful.

137. Once the Holy Prophet (p.b.u.h.) told his Companion Hazrat Abu Hurairah (r.a.) that spiritual and moral decline of the Muslims would start by 60 A.H.

Hazrat Abu Hurairah (r.a.) says:

"I used to wish publicly that I might not live to see 60 A.H."

He died in 59 A.H. Moreover, the prediction of the Apostle came true with the coming of Yazeed on the throne.

138. ***Mukhtar And Hajjaj:***

The Holy Prophet (p.b.u.h.) had once said that there would be born a 'lier' and a "killer" in the Thaqeef tribe.

When Hajjaj Thaqafee hanged Hazrat Abdullah bin Zubair (r.a.), he sent for his (Abdullah bin Zubair's) mother, Hazrat Asmaa (r.a.). But she refused the summons.

At last Hajjaj himself called on Hazrat Asmaa (r.a.) she said to him:

"Mukhttar Thaqafee was known as a "liar" and that, according to the prophecy of the Prophet (p.b.u.h.), she thought that Hajjaj was the "killer."

On hearing this, Hajjaj went away without saying a word.

139. ***Four Periods:***

Once the Holy Prophet (p.b.u.h.) had declared publicly that there were four periods — his own time, one after that, then after that and followed by another — when people would give evidence at their own initiative without being called; who would be guilty of misappropriations; who would not be trustworthy; who would not keep their promises.

The four periods mentioned by the Holy Prophet (p.b.u.h.) were: The period of the Apostle himself; that of his Companions (Sahaba); that of the Tabi'yeen; and the one of the Taba-tabiyeen.

These four periods were productive of the moral, and religious excellence of the Muslims. They produced pious persons , Imams and great spiritual leaders one after another. In these periods Islam was at its peak.

Thereafter, Islam went on declining day by day. Innovations were introduced, oppression started, evil acts prevailed, learned persons became victims of false desires. Philosphies of Greece,India and Persia exerted influences among the Muslims bringing about weaknesses in the beliefs, creeds and deeds of the Muslims as a whole, with the result Islam saw disorder and general disorganisation.

140. ***Women In Business:***

Once the Holy Prophet (p.b.u.h.) had predicted that a time would come when even women would take part in business and trade with men that business would be a widely practised profession.

141. ***The World Against The Muslims:***

The Holy Prophet (p.b.u.h.) had once predicted that a time would come when the nations of the world would unite against the

Muslims, although they would be large in number. He added that they would fall victim because of their involvement with the world, fear of death. Fears of the Muslims will leave the hearts of the unbelievers.

We now see the prediction of the Apostle come true.

142. ***The Four Caliphs:***

Once Ibn Haban said to Safina, the freed man of the Holy Prophet (p.b.u.h.) that when the Apostle started construction of the Mosque in Madina, he laid the foundation stone himself and then asked Abu Bakr (R.A.) to put his stone. Thereafter Umar and Usman (R.A.) were asked to do the same in succession.

The above-mentioned tradition was reported by Hakam and Baihaqie. And the Caliphs of the Faithfuls Abu Bakr, Umar and Uthman took charge in the same order.

143. ***Hakam Reports Hazrat Anas (r.a.) (noted servant of the Apostle) to have said:***

"Once he was sent by Bani al-Mustaliq to the Holy Prophet (p.b.u.h.) to inquire of him on their behalf that to whom should they take their presents to after him; so he came to the Apostle and asked him the question.

"To Abu Bakr," the Holy Prophet (p.b.u.h.) replied. When he informed them to what the Apostle had said, they again sent him to ask the Apostle as to what should they do in case anything ill befalls Abu bakr (r.a.)?

"To Umar," the Apostle replied.

They again sent him to the Holy Prophet (p.b.u.h.) to ask that if something serious by dangerous befell Umar (r.a.), then whom should they go with their presents to?

"To Osman?" the Holy Prophet (p.b.u.h.) replied.

When they sent him again to the Holy Prophet (p.b.u.h.) to ask what should they do in case a peril befalls to Osman?

"If peril befalls Osman, then there will be ruin and destruction, and so forth,' the Apostle said in reply.

144. ***Once Hazrat Abu Hurairah (r.a.) saw the following in dream:***

"I was on a well and there was a bucket on it also. I drew as much water out of the well as it pleased Almighty Allah. Thereafter Abu Bakr took the bucket and with ease drew one or two bucketful of water. The bucket then became a large one and it was taken by Omar ibn Khattab (r.a.). I never saw such a strong person drawing out water. Now the people were fully satisfied with water while there were multitudes of them around the well.

145. ***Abu Dawud and Hakam report from Jabbar bin Abdullah that once the Holy Prophet (p.b.u.h.) said:-***

"A righteous person saw in a dream that Abu Bakr was suspended with the Apostle and Omar with Abu Bakr and Osman with Umar."

Jabir goes on to say that when he and others left the Holy Prophet (p.b.u.h.) they said among themselves:

"The righteous person who dreamt was the Prophet himself and the suspension of one with the other signified that they should be inheritors of the trust for which Allah had sent the Apostle, and so forth."

146. ***Hakam cites Safina as saying:***

"It was a habit of the Prophet (p.b.a.h.) every day after the morning prayers to ask his companions if any one of them had a dream. Once a certain person told him that he had dreamt as if a balance descended from above and that the Apostle was put in one pan of it and Abu Bakr in the other, that the Apostle's pan was heavier; then Umar was put against Abu Bakr in the other pan, Abu Bakr's pan proved heavier; and then was put Osman against Umar and Umar's pan counter poised. The balance was then drawn up again: on hearing this the complexion of the Apostle's countenance was changed and he said: "The Caliphate would last for thirty years only and the monarchy would prevail."

146. ***Abu Dawud cites from Samura bin Jundab (r.a.) that a man said to the Holy Prophet (p.b.u.h.):***

"O Prophet of Allah, I saw in a dream that something like a bucket was hung from the heaven, and then came Abu Bakr (r.a.) and held the bucket by its strings and drank a little water; then Umar came and caught the bucket by its ropes and drank to his fill and then came Osman and did the same and was amply satisfied. Thereafter Ali did the same, but the strings of the bucket were to loose and a little water fell upon Ali."

147. ***Hazrat Anas bin Malik reports:***

"Once the Holy Prophet (p.b.u.h..) ascended the hill Uhad accompanied by Abu Bakr, Umar and Osman. The hill began to shake and shook them also. The Apostle stamped it and asked it to be at rest and said to it that there were on it one Prophet, one 'Siddeeq' (truthful) and two 'Shaheeds' (martyrs). By the Prophet he meant himself; by the Siddiq, Abu Bakr; and by the two martyrs,, Umar and Osman." (Bukhari).

148. ***Hazrat Abu Musa Ash'ari (r.a.) reports:***

"Once I was with the Holy Prophet (p.b.u.h.) in one of the gardens of Madina. In the meantime, a certain person came and wished the gate opened: The Apostle directed me to open the gate and give the comer the good news of the Paradise. I opened the gate and saw Abu Bakr, whom I gave the glad tidings as ordered by the Apostle. He thanked and praised Allah (Bukhari, Muslim).

149. ***Abu Huraira reports:***

"Once the Holy Prophet (p.b.u.h.) was on Mount Haray and there were with him Abu Bakr, Osman, Ali, Talha and Zubair. The rock shook and the Apostle commanded it to be at rest for there were on it none else but the Prophet, the Siddeeq, and the martyrs." (Muslim). The prediction came true later on.

150. Imam Ahmed, Tirmizi, Ibn Majah and Hakam report from Hazrat Aisha (r.a.) that once the Holy Prophet (p.b.u.h.) told Osman (r.a.).

"O Osman: certainly Allah will put on you a chemise, which you, though the antagonisms might wish you to do so, should not put off till you meet me'

In this tradition, the chemise typifies the Caliphate and Osman is warned that Allah would give Caliphate to him and that if the unbelievers should desire a portion of the Caliphate he should not mind them and should not severe from the Caliphate till death; and so it came to pass that Osman became the Caliph and the unbelievers demanded a portion of the Caliphate, but he did not, according to the direction of the Holy Prophet (p.b.u.h.), accept their proposals, but told them he was content with the agreement which the Apostle made him to make.

151. ***Tirmizi cites from Abdullah ibn Omar (r.a.):***

"Once the Holy Prophet (p.b.u.h.) made mention of a quarrel and pointing to Osman (r.a.) said that he would be innocently killed in it."

And so it came to pass that Osman (r.a.) was faultlessly slain in an uproar of the Egyptians and the Iraqis.

152. ***Baihaqi reports;***

One day the Holy Prophet (p.b.u.h.) saw Ali and Zubair laughing together and he asked Ali if he loved Zubair. Ali replied how could he not love Zubair who was his aunt's son and his co-religionist. The Apostle then asked Zubair if he loved Ali, he replied how could he do otherwise he being his uncle's son and his co-religionist. Thereupon the Holy Prophet (p.b.u.h.) told Zubair that it would soon happen that he would wage war with Ali and that he would be the aggressor."

The prediction came true at the Battle of Jamal when Ali and Zubair came face to face. Hazrat Ali (r.a.) made him swear and asked him if he had not heard the Apostle say that he would wage war against him and that he would prove cruel. Zubair said:

"Certainly I had heard but I had forgotten."

Saying this Zubair retreated from the battlefield.

153. ***Imam Ahmed reports from Ali (r.a.):***

"Once the Holy Prophet (p.b.u.h.) told him that your case would be like Jesus, whom the Jews took as their enemy so far that they blamed his mother and the Christians took as a friend so far they exalted him to a position which did not belong to him.

So in your case, there would be exaggerations too; some people would become enemical to you and would depreciate you so much as to talk ill of you and accuse you falsely, and some people would befriend you and extol you so far that you would not merit it, they would call you God."

And so it was, that there crept in discrepancies about Ali. The Nawasib and Khwarij talk ill of him and accuse him of ill-treatment with Aisha and accessary to the murder of Osman, and the Rafizi congregations call him God.

154. ***Imam Ahmed reports:***

"Once the Holy Prophet (p.b.u.h.) asked Umar ibn Khattab (r.a.) if he knew who of the ancient religious sects was the most wretched and who is the most wretched of our sect. Umar (r.a.) said that the most wretched of the former sects was the ruddy man of Samaod tribe, i.e., Qudar bin Salif who cut the tendons of the leg of Naqatullah, and the most wretched of our sect is the man who would give sword-cut on your pate so that your beard would be drenched with blood and the sword should make a martyr," In this tradition the Holy Prophet (p.b.u.h.) foretells that the executioner of Ali (r.a.) shall inflict a sword wound on his head and that the blood shall redden his beard and that he shall thereby be martyred, and so it came to pass that Abdul Rahman bin Maljam Kharji smote his forehead with a sword in the morning and blood flowed down his beard and he was therefrom made a martyr.

Through the conversation of the Prophet (p.b.u.h.), Ali (r.a.) was made so fully acquainted with the circumstances of his martydom that in the night preceding the morning when Ibn Maljam would attack him Ali (r.a.) came out several times and gazed upon the sky and said: By Allah, he never told a lie, nor a lie was ever told to him, that it was the same night of which a promise was given him: and at dawn the geese began to crackle before him, the people drove them away. But he told them to let them alone for they lamented. The "muaz'zin" then came and told him of prayer. He came out to lead the prayer. Ibn Maljam was sleeping in the mosque. Hazrat Ali (r.a.) got him awakened and himself engaged in prayer. Ibn Maljam got up and as Hazrat Ali (r.a.) lay in prostration, he struck forcefully at his head so that a very deep injury was inflicted and blood flowed down his beard turning it red. Thus the prediction of the Holy Prophet (p.b.u.h.) about Ali came true.

155. ***Imam Ahmed and Baihaqi report from Huzaifa:***

"Once the Holy Prophet (p.b.u.h.) said that there should be a prophetic age among you as long as Allah would wish, and then He would remove it. Thereafter Caliphatic age would start for a time as Allah would wish; and this should also be removed by Allah when He would like, then it should be supplanted by an iron monarchy which should last and be removed as Allah would be pleased; and after monarchy the caliphate should prevail after the prophetic fashion, and then the Prophet (p.b.u.h.) became silent."

Habib the transcriber of this tradition reports that when Umar bin Abdul Azeez became the Caliph of Islam, he sent him a copy of this tradition writing that on the expiration of the cruel and biting monarchy he would be the chosen Caliph, on hearing this he praised Almighty Allah.

Thus the prophecy of the Holy Prophet (p.b.u.h.) came true. After the demise of the Prophet (p.b.u.h.) the prophetic age came to an end; then began the era of four Caliphs one after another. It was followed by an oppressive and iron monarchy. Thereafter prophetic type of Caliphate was restored once again when Umar bin Abdul Azeez became the Caliph.

156. ***Thoban reports the following:***

"Once the Holy Prophet (p.b.u.h.) said that Almighty Allah gathered the whole land and showed it eastern and western ends to him. Thereafter he added: as far as he saw the sovereignty of his followers would cover these areas."

And accordingly, it came to pass that in a very short period, that is during the Caliphate age the extent of the kingdom of the followers of the Prophet had so widened and enlarged that no other king on the face of the earth had so much territory. And till the days of Osman (R.A.) the breadth of the Muslim empire stretched from Constantinople to Aden, and the length from Indus to Balkh. (Muslim).

157. ***In Sahihain there is a tradition as reported by Sa'ad bin Abi Waqqas (r.a.):***

"I was sick in Mak'kah on the occasion of Hajjat-ul-Wida, and the Holy Prophet (p.b.u.h.) went to see him. I thought that I would die of that malady. I, therefore, prayed the Apostle that my heir would be my only daughter and I would, therefore, bequeath two-thirds of my having towards charity or alms. But the Apostle declined the proposal. I then said about 'half' but received the same answer; whereupon I said 'one-third' and the Apostle asserted.

Thereafter the Holy Prophet (p.b.u.h.) predicted that he hoped I would live so long that many others should derive great benefit through me and many more suffered injuries."

In this prophecy the Holy Prophet (p.b.u.h.) foretold that Sa'ad bin Abi Waqqas should be cured of his illness and he could live so long that many a man should have good and bad at his hands. And so it happened that after the recovery from illness he lived more than fifty years and the Muslims were benefited plentiful by him and the infidel Magies were subjected to great losses.

In the Caliphate of Hazrat Umar ibn Khattab (R:A.) Persia was vanquished by him; and that great battle of Qadsia was won by him: In this battle 32,000 Muslims and a lac and a half of Magies were engaged, Rustam bin Farakhzad was made the Magain Commander by Yazdgird, the king of Persia. Rustam was slain and Median, the ancient capital of the Iranian kings came to Muslim possession, and immense treasures of the Iranian Emperors were transferred to the Muslim.

The infidel Magies were inflicted great losses by Sa'ad bin Abi Waq'qas (r.a.) because thousands of them were slain and hundreds made slaves and their country and treasures were snatched from them. Thus the prophecy of the Holy Prophet (p.b.u.h.) proved to be correct.

158. ***Six Incidents Before the Last Day:-***

Bukhari reports from Auf bin Malik:

"I came to the Holy Prophet (p.b.u.h.) during the Battle of Tabuk, when he was in a tent of leather. He told me to court six incidents before the Last Day:

1. my death; 2. the conquest of the holy city Jerusalem; 3. an epidemic among them like that of goats; 4. abundance of riches so that a man would not gladly accept 100 dinars if he is given; 5. a meeting to be joined by all Arab families without exception; 6. there would be a treaty between Nasaras (Christians) and them which they would break leading to war."

Ist, the conquest of Jerusalem after the demise of the Holy Prophet (p.b.u.h.): It came to pass during the Caliphate of Hazrat Ubaida bin Jarrah, the Commander of Syrian Army during the Caliphate of Umar (r.a.) beseiged the Holy city, there was in the fort a bishop, who said to Ubaida (r.a.) on seeing his face that the fort was to be conquered by him; that the name and speciality of the conqueror was with one whose name was Umar. Ubaida informed Umar of this. Hence Umar ibn Khattab (r.a.) went to Jerusalem in person and the bishop in looking at his face said that he was the man appointed to subdue the stronghold and immediately he caused the castle to be evacuated. So from this conquest of Jerusalem two proofs of Muhammad (p.b.u.h.) being Prophet are seen: (a) occuring of things accordingly as they were foretold; and (b) that a detailed account of the Prophet and his companions had been given in former scriptures. 2nd, the prevalence of an epidemic after the conquest of Jerusalem: it also happened in 16 A.H. near Jerusalem where the forces of Abu Ubaida were encanyed such a virulent pestilence broke out that 70,000 men died in three days and Abu Ubaida (r.a.) died in the same epidemic.

3rd, the plenteousness of wealth: This also came to be the state during the days of the leading Caliphs especially in the Caliphate of Osman (r.a.).

4th, a great rebellions warfare which should possess all the Arab clans. This refers to the uprising against Osman (r.a.) which caused horrible strifes and slaughter among the Muslims, and hardly anybody escaped this catastrophe.

5th, the conclusion of a treaty between the Muslim and the Christians, and then its violation by the latter and their invasion upon the former which forms the 6th prediction of the Apostle.

159. ***Bukhari quotes Umm-i-Haram (r.a.) as reporting:***

"One day the Holy Prophet (p.b.u.h.) slept at my residence and awaked laughing. I asked him the reason of his laughter. He (the Apostle) said that he saw in the dream that his Companions sailed in ships for `jihad.' I said, `O Prophet of Allah, may I be among those crusaders?" The Apostle replied, "you are already among them." Thereafter the Apostle slept again and re-awaked laughing. I asked again the reason of his laughter. He replied, "The first army that would wage war with the Roman Emperor would have its sin forgiven." Here the Holy Prophet (p.b.u.h.) foretold of three things: First, of the crusade by his followers in the Mediterranean; second, the inclusion of Umm-i-Haram among the crusaders against Constantinople, the capital of Roman Empire.

160. ***Reconciliation between two groups:***

Bukhari quotes from Hazrat Abu Bakr (r.a.)

"Once the Prophet from (p.b.u.h.) pointing to Hasan (r.a.) said that his son was Saiyed and that it is hoped that through him Allah will bring about a reconciliation between two great multitudes of Muslims." This prophecy came true when after the martyrdom of Hazrat Ali (r.a.) the Muslims swore allegiance to Hazrat Hasan (r.a.) and he was made the Caliph. Later a battle took place between the soldiers of Hasan (r.a.) and Amir Muawiyya. Hazrat Hasan (r.a.) presuming bloodshed of the Muslims on a large scale on both sides, entered into a peace treaty and thus became an instrument of peace and tranquility to Muslims.

161. ***Baihaqee reports from Umm-ul-Fazl:***

"Once I came before the Apostle and said that I had a very bad dream. The Holy Prophet (p.b.u.h.) asked me about the dream. I narrated that a part of my blessed body severed and fell into my lap. Thereupon the Apostle revealed that the dream had a good news. It meant that Fatima should give birth to a son who would be in her lap. Accordingly, Imam Husain was born and was put in my lap. Thus the prophecy of the Holy Prophet (p.b.u.h.) came true."

162. ***Baihaqee reports from Umm-e-Fazl:***

"Once I had Imam Husain in my lap that the Holy Prophet (p.b.u.h.) came and staring him burst into tears. I requested him to give the reason of his shedding tears. Thereupon, the Apostle revealed that Jibrail (Gabriel) had informed him that his followers would kill his son, Husain."

Later Imam Husain was slain in Kerbala making the prophecy true."

163. ***Abu Noam reports:***

"Once I was with Ali and Imam Husain in the Saqar Safeen. When we came to the town of Tainvi, Ali warned Husain to stop on the banks of the Euphrates. When I asked the reason, Ali revealed that he had been forewarned by Jibrail that Husain should be killed on the banks of the Euphrates, and he (the Apostle) had been shown a handful of dust of that place by the arch angel."

164. ***Ibn-i-Asakar reports from Mohammad bin Umar bin Hasan:***

"Once I was with Imam Husain in the Kerbala. The Imam said on seeing Shimar, 'Allah and his Messenger told the truth." On enquiry he revealed, "The Holy Prophet (p.b.u.h.) told that he saw a white-spotted dog putting his snout in the blood of his skin; and Shimar had white leprosy and was spotted white.

165. ***Hazrat A'isha (r.a.) reports:***

"Once the Holy Prophet (p.b.u.h.,) told his chaste wives that among us she should meet him (the Apostle) first whose hands were the longest. We (the wives) conjectured what the length of the hand meant. We measured the length of our hands with a stick.

But when Zainab died we came to the conclusion that by large hand the Holy Prophet (p.b.u.h.) meant munificence, alms-giving, charity, etc. Since Zainab excelled all in these qualities, the prophecy of the Apostle came true." (Sahihain).

166. ***Abu Naim reports from Ibn-i-Abbas:***

"Once my mother, Umm-ul-Fazl, passed in front of the Holy Prophet (p.b.u.h.). He called her and revealed that from that conception of hers she should bear a son and when the boy should be born, she should bring him to him. Thus when I was born she took me to the Apostle who called "Azan" in the right ear and "aqamat" in the left one. Thereafter he tasted me his spittle of the mouth and named me, "Abdullah." then he asked my mother to take me away --- the father of the Caliphs.

When my mother narrated the matter to my father Abbas, he went to the Apostle and mentioned what he heard from his father. The Holy Prophet (p.b.u.h.) told him that the boy was in reality the Father of the caliphs."

The prophecy of the Holy Prophet (p.b.u.h.) proved to be correct because the Abbaside Caliphate had been in ascendancy for five hundred years.

167. ***Prophecies About The Results Of The Battles:***

Urwah and Sa'eed bin Mus'ab report:

"The Holy Prophet (p.b.u.h.) had told Abi bin Khalaf that he would be killed by him (the Prophet)."

"The prophecy came true in that he was wounded by the Apostle and died of the wound. (Baihaqee). It is narrated that Abi bin Khalaf was too deadly inimical to the Prophet to have a horse whom he gave gram and grass saying that mounting on it he might slay him.

When the Messenger of Allah heard, he replied, 'if Allah so pleased, he (the Apostle) would kill him."

Now during the Battle of Uhad, Abi bin Khalaf challenged by saying, "Where is Muhammad, today he will not be spared from his hand." While he was advancing, the Companions of the Apostle wanted to prevent him. But the Holy Prophet (p.b.u.h.) said, "Let him come." When he came close, the Apostle hit him with a lance taken from a Companion. The lance hit an exposed part of his chin and inflicted a scratching wound which did not even bleed; but he fell down his horse and ran towards the Qurashi'ite. When they told him that there was no danger to him, he replied that the wound was from none but Muhammad's hands, and he would not remain alive even if he spat upon him. And, accordingly, he died on his way to Mak'kah.

168. ***Abi Qatada reports:***

"During the Battle of Trench Amaar bin Yaser was digging a trench that the Holy Prophet (p.b.u.h.) moved his hand over his head and said:

"Regretful, a band of rebels shall kill thee, O son of Sumaiya."

The above prophecy came true in the Battle of Siffin when Amaar bin Yaser was slain by the force of Muawiya. (Muslim).

169. During the days of Ignorance, Ka'aba used to be opened on Mondays and Thursday. The key of Ka'aba remained in the possession of Uthman bin Talha.

One day the Holy Prophet (p.b.u.h.) wanted to enter it for prayer. But Uthman refused to open the door of Ka'aba and uttered harsh words. The Apostle listened all patiently, and said to Uthman bin Talha:

"One day you shall see that key in my possession and I may give it to anyone I will like."

Thereupon Uthman replied,

"Shall the Quraishi'ite become extinct and disparaged that day?"

"That day the Quraishi'ite shall be more exalted," said the Holy Prophet (p.b.u.h.) in reply.

On the day of the conquest of Mak'kah, the Messenger of Allah sent for Uthman bin Talha, and he came before the Apostle with the key of Ka'aba." (Tabqat-Ibn Sa'd).

In the above tradition there are two prophecies of the Holy Prophet (p.b.u.h.) proving to be correct.

Firstly, that one day the key of Ka'aba shall be in his hand. Secondly, the Prophet of Islam while giving back the key of Ka'aba to Uthman had predicted that it should remain with his family in future too. Now the second prophecy also came true as the key was still in possession of the family of Uthman bin Talha.

170. ***Sahl bin Hanzala reports:***

"A cavalier came to the Prophet (p.b.u.h.) during the Battle of Hunain that he ascended a certain hill and saw that the whole Hawazin clan came to Hunain with their camels and cattle. Thereupon the Messenger of Allah smiled and said:

"The next day if Allah be pleased, all that would be the booty of the Muslims." (Abu Dawood).

The prophecy came true the day following. The Battle of Hunain was won with a large booty that fell into the hands of the Believers.

171. When the Holy Prophet (p.b.u.h.) sent Hazrat Khalid bin Waleed (r.a.) against Ukaider, Governor of Damat-ul-Jandal, he had already told Khalid that Ukaider would surrender to him.

Hazrat Khalid bin Waleed, Commander of the Islamic Army arrived at the fort of Ukaider bin Abdul Mulk in a moon-lit night. Ukaider was very fond of Neelghan hunting. When he was reeling over his balcony in that moon-lit night, some Neelghans came to the wall of his stronghold and began to rub themselves with the wall of the fortress.

On hearing the whiz so produced he looked down and found four animals near the fort. He rushed towards the animals with his brother Hassaun to hunt them as soon as possible. Khalid was waiting for the opportunity. As he came out of the fort, Khalid fell upon him suddenly and made him a captive; while his brother was killed. Ukaider was produced before the Messenger of Allah, was left after being levelled Islamic tax upon him." (Baihaqee and Ibn Ishaq).

172. ***Praying for Rain in Madina:***

Hazrat Anas (r.a.) reports:

"Once the people of Madina were afflicted by famine during the lifetime of the Holy Prophet (p.b.u.h.). Now when the Apostle was delivering his Friday sermon, a nomadic Arab got up and said:

"O Prophet of Allah! the animals are perishing and the children are hungry; so make supplication to Allah for us."

Thereupon the Messenger of Allah raised his hands at once. While there was not a speck of cloud in the sky, but I swear by Allah in whose hand my soul is, that he had not lowered his hand before the clouds were appearing like mountains and before he descended from his pulpit, I saw the rain coming down on his beard.

We had rain that day, the next, the following day, and till the next Friday. Then (during the Friday Sermon) that nomadic Arab or someone else got up and said, "O Messenger of Allah! the buildings are being broken down and the animals are being drowned, so make supplication to Allah for us."

The Apostle then raised his hands and said:

"O Allah! (Send rain) round about us, but not on us."

The Messenger of Allah did not point to any region in the clouds without their breaking up; and Madina became like gap. The "wadi" (valley) had a channel flowing in it for a month, and no one came from any region without speaking of plenty." (Bukhari; Muslim)

173. ***A Jew Converted to Islam:***

Hazrat Anas (r.a.) reports:

"Once a learned Jew `Abdullah bin Salam came to know that the Messenger of Islam had arrived. He was then in his orchard gathering dates. He left his work, appeared before the Prophet of Islam and said:

"I shall ask you about three things which only a prophet knows. What is the first sign of the Last Hour? What is the first things the inhabitants of Paradise will eat? What makes a baby look like its father or its mother?"

The Messenger of Allah replied:

"Jibrail has just informed me about them (i.e., your questions). The first sign of the Last Hour will be a fire which will drive mankind from the east to the west. The first thing the inhabitants of Paradise will eat will be the liver of a fish. When liquid of the man comes before the woman's, he attracts the child to his likeness; but when the liquid of the woman comes first it attracts it to her likeness."

Thereupon Abdullah bin Salam said."

"I testify that only Allah has the right to be worshipped and that you are Messenger of Allah. O Apostle! the Jews are slanderous people, and if they know of my acceptance of Islam before you ask them will slander me."

When the Jews came, the Holy Prophet (p.b.u.h.) asked:

"What kind of man is Abdullah among you?"

"Our best one and the son of our best one, our chief and the son of our chief," they replied.

"Tell me what you will do if he accepts Islam." the Apostle asked, "May Allah preserve him."

Thereupon Abdullah came out and said:

"I testify that none has right to be worshipped but Allah, and that Muhammad is the Messenger of Allah."

They said:

"He is the worst of us and the son of the worst of us."

"This is what I feared, O `Messenger of Allah,"

Abdullah bin Salam said.

174. ***Speaking of a Wolf:***

Hazrat Abu Hurairah (r.a.) reports:

"A wolf came and took away a sheep. The sheperd ran after it and snatched it from it. Thereafter the wolf climbed on a mound and having sat on its haunches with its tail between its legs said, "I took the sheep as a provision of Allah but you snatched that from me." The shepherd wondered at the sight and said,"By Allah, I have never seen like it before, a wolf talking."

"But more wonderful is the man among the palm-trees between the two "harras" who can tell what has already happened and what is going to be happened after your time," the wolf replied.

The shepherd was a Jew. Having heard from the wolf, he came to the Holy Prophet (p.b.u.h.) and embraced Islam. (Sharh-al-Sunnah).

175. ***Unais bin 'Amr reports:***

"Ahban bin Aus narrates, "I was amongst my sheep. All of a sudden a wolf appeared and caught a sheep. Thereupon I shouted at it at the top of my voice. At this the wolf sat on its tail and addressed me, saying:

"Who will look after the sheep when you are busy and not able to look after it? How can you forbid me the provision which Allah, the Almighty has kept for me?"

Ahban further said, "clapping with both hands I said with wonder that I had never seen something more wonderful and striking during my whole life."

"But there is something more wonderful than this." the wolf said with confidence and added, "It is this that the Prophet of Allah is inviting people to Almighty Allah."

"Hearing this, Ahban went to Allah's Apostle and informing him about his wonderful site, accepted Islam."

'Amr said. (Fatah al-Bari).

176. ***Prayer Granted:***

Abdullah bin 'Amr (r.a.) reports:

"The Holy Prophet (p.b.u.h.) went out at the Battle of Badr with his three hundred and thirteen Companions. Most of them were in a very wretched condition. The Messenger of Allah felt disturbed at their state of life and their sacrifice for the cause of Almighty Allah, and raised his hands in prayer, saying:

"O Allah they are hungry, so satiate them; they are naked, so clothe them; they are bare-footed, so provide mount for them.

Allah, the Exalted bestowed victory on them and almost all his Companions went back home with provision, cloth and camels. (Abu Dawud).

177. ***Calling the Dead:***

Anas (r.a.) reports Hazrat Umar (r.a.) to have narrated:

"After the Battle of Badr, the slain among the unbelievers were put into a well on top of one another. After sometime the Holy Prophet (p.b.u.h.) went near the well and called, "So and so and son of so and so! have you found true what your deities had promised you to be?" I have found true what my Allah had promised me to be true?" Thereupon I (Umar) asked the Messenger of Allah, "How can you speak to bodies which contain no spirits?"

The Apostle replied:

"You are no better able to hear what I am saying than they are but they are unable to make any reply."(Muslim).

178. ***Fighting Right and Left:***

Hazrat Sa'd bin Abi Waqqas (r.a.) reports:

"During the Battle of Uhad I saw two men in spotless white dress whom I had never seen before. I saw them fighting right and left of the Messenger of Allah. I was later told that they were Jibrail and Mikail."(Bukhari, Muslim).

179. ***Putting off Armour:***

Hazrat Ai'sha (r.a.) reports:

"After coming back from the Battle of the Trench the Holy Prophet (p.b.u.h.) put off his armour and took bath. When the Apostle was rubbing his head, Jibrail came to him and said:

"You have put off your armour, but I swear by Allah, that the angels have not done so, hence go out to them." On enquiry Jibrail revealed, "To Bani Quraiza."

Hence the Messenger of Allah went to them (Bukhari; Muslim).

180. ***Truths Revealed:***

Hazrat Abu Hurairah (r.a.) reports:

"After the conquest of Khaiber a poisoned sheep was presented to the Holy Prophet (p.b.u.h.) by the Jews. Thereupon the Messenger of Allah asked to collect the Jews present there. When the Jews assembled, the Apostle said to them:

"I am going to ask you something, so will you tell me the truth about it?"

"Yes, Abul QAsim," they replied with one voice.

"Who was their father?" the Apostle asked.

"He was so and so," they replied.

"No their was so and so and that they were telling a lie," said the Prophet of Allah.

"Thou have spoken the truth," they admitted.

"Will you tell me the truth about a matter I ask you about?, the Prophet of Allah asked.

"Yes, Abul QAsim; and if we tell a lie, you will come to know the truth as you did in case of our father," they replied.

"Who will go to hell," the Apostle asked.

"We shall be in the hell for a time being, then you will go to hell." they replied.

"Go off in shame into the hell. I swear by Allah that we will never succeed you in it,"said the Apostle.

"Will you tell me the truth about a matter if I ask you about it? the Apostle said.

"Yes, Abul QAsim," they replied.

"Have you put poison in this sheep?" the Apostle said.

"Yes, we did so," they replied.

"What had induced you to do so?" the Prophet asked.

"We wanted to get rid of you in case you are a liar;

and as you are telling the truth it will not harm you," they replied. (Bukhari).

181. ***Prediction of Sorrows:***

Abu Wa'il reports from Hudhaifa:

"Who amongst you remembers the statement of the Messenger of Allah regarding the afflictions?" once Hazrat Umar ibn Khattab (r.a.) asked.

"I remember what did the Apostle said about it," said Hudhaifa.

"Tell, you are really a darling man," Hazrat Umar said.

"The Messenger of Allah had said that a man's afflictions

regarding his family, his property and his neighbours are expiated by his prayers, charities and enjoining what is good and forbidding what is bad," Hudhaifa replied.

"I don't mean these afflictions but the afflictions that will be heaving up and down like waves of the sea," Hazrat Umar said.

"O chief of the Believers! you need not fear those afflictions as there is a closed door between you and them," Hudhaifa replied.

"Will that door be opened or broken?" Hazrat Umar asked.

"It will be broken," Hudhaifa replied.

"Then it is very likely that the door will not be closed again," Hazrat Umar replied.

Later on the people asked Hudhaifa, "Did Hazrat Umar know what that door actually meant?"

"Yes, Umar knew it as everyone knows that tonight precedes tomorrow and I had narrated to Umar something authentic and not a lie," Hudhaifa said.

"We dared not ask Hudhaifa," said Abu Wa'il. However he added that once they asked Masruq about it who had asked Hudhaifa about the matter.

When asked, 'what does the door stand for?"

"Umar," was the reply from Masruq. (Bukhari).

182. ***Ibn Mas'ud (r.a.) reports the Holy Prophet (p.b.u.h.) to have said:***

"Very soon others will be preferred to you; and you will come across things you will not like."

"O Messenger of Allah, what do you enjoin us to do in such a case?" the Companions of the Apositle asked.

"Give the rights that are on you and ask your rights from Allah," the Prophet of Allah replied. (Bukhari)

183. ***Usama (r.a.) reports:***

"Once the Holy Prophet (p.b.u.h.) stood on one of the high buildings (of Madina) and said:

"Do you see what I see?" and added, "I see afflictions pouring down your houses like rain drops."(Bukhari)

184. ***Uqba bin 'Amr (r.a.) reports:***

"Once the Holy Prophet (p.b.u.h.) offered the funeral prayer for the martyrs of Uhud, and thereafter proceeding to the pulpit he said:

"I shall be your predecessor and a witness on you; and I am really looking at my sacred Fount now. No doubt, I have been given the key of the treasures of the world. By Allah, I am not afraid that you will worship others alongwith Allah, but I am afraid that you will envy and fight each other for worldly fortunes." (Bukhari)

185. ***Zainab bint Jahsh (r.a.) reports:***

"Once the Holy Prophet (p.b.u.h.) came to me in a state of fear and said:

"None has the right to be worshipped but Allah! Woe to the Arabs because of evil that has come near. Today a hole has been in the wall of Gog and Magog as large as this," pointing with two of his fingers making a circle."

"O Messenger of Allah! Shall we be destroyed though amongst us there are pious people?" "Yes, if evil increases," The Apostle said.

186 ***Hazrat Umm Salama reports***:

"Once the Holy Prophet (p.b.u.h.) woke up and said: Glorified be Allah! What great treasures have been sent down, and what great afflictions have been sent down!" (Bukhari)

187. ***The Day of Resurrection Predicted:***

Hazrat Amr bin Akhtab al-Ansari reports:

"One day the Messenger of Allah led us in the `Fajr' (dawn) prayer, and mounting the pulpit addressed us till the `Zuhar' (noon) prayer.

Thereafter he descended from the pulpit, led the prayer and again mounted the pulpit and addressed us till the 'Asr' (afternoon) prayer. He then descended and led the prayer.

After that he ascended the pulpit and addressed us till the sunset. In his addresses the Messenger of Allah informed us of what is to happen up to the day of Resurrection. (Muslim)

188. *Hazrat Ali (r.a.) reports:*

"I relate the tradition of the Messenger of Allah to you; for I would rather fall from the sky than attribute anything to him (the Apostle) falsely. Once I heard the Holy Prophet (p.b.u.h.) saying:

"In the last days of this world, there will appear some foolish people who will use the best speech (the Qur'an) for their own ends. Their faith will not go beyond their throats (i.e.), they will have practically no belief); so wherever you find them, kill them; for he who kills them shall gain a reward on the Day of Resurrection." (Bukhari.)

189. ***Hazrat Abu Hurairah (r.a.) reports the Messenger of Allah to have said:***

"The Day of Resurrection will not be established till there is a war between two groups inflicting great number of casualties, although claiming the same faith.

And the Hour will not be established till there appear about thirty liars claiming to be the messengers of Allah." (Bukhari).

190. ***Hazrat Abu Hurairah (r.a.) reports the Messenger of Allah to have said:***

"The Day of Resurrection will not be established till you fight a nation wearing hairy shoes, and till you fight the Turks, who will have small eyes, red faces and flat noses; and their faces will be like flat shields.

And you will find that the best people are those who hate responsibility of ruling most of all till they are chosen to be the rulers." (Bukhari).

191. ***Predicting Death:***

Hazrat Abdullah ibn Abbas (r.a.) reports:

"In his fatal illness, the Holy Prophet (p.b.u.h.) came out, wrapped with a sheet and wrapping his head with an oily bandage. He sat on the pulpit, and praising and glorifying Allah, the Almighty, he said:

"From now on people will increase but the Ansar will decrease in number, so much so that they will remain just like salt in the meals. So, if anyone of you achieves power by which you can benefit some and harm others; it is better to favour their virtues and excuse their faults." (Bukhari).

192. ***Predicting Future:***

Hazrat Abu Hurairah (R.A.) reports:

"Once the Holy Prophet (p.b.u.h.) predicted the following:

"When Khosroes perishes, there will be no (more) Khosroes after him; and when Caesar perishes, there will be no (more) Caesar after him. By Him in whose Hands Muhammad's life is, you will spend the treasures of both of them in the Cause of Allah, the Almighty." (Bukhari).

193. ***Hazrat Hudhaifa (r.a.) reports the Holy Prophet (p.b.u.h.) to have said:***

"Among my Companions (or people according to another version), there will be twelve hypocrites who will neither enter paradise nor have its odour. Eight of them will be repelled by an internal ulcer which will appear on their shoulders and extend into their breasts." (Muslim).

194. ***Hazrat Khabbab bin al-Aratt (r.a.) reports:***

"One day the Holy Prophet (p.b.u.h.) was lying on a stripped cloak in the shade of the Ka'aba. We complained him against the persecution from polytheists and requested him to make supplication to Allah."

Thereupon the Apostle's face turned red and he sat straight to say:

"Before your time a man was put in a pit dug for him, then his head was cut in two with a saw, but those sufferings and miseries failed to turn him away from his Faith. Another person was combed with iron combs below his flesh, but he did not break with his Faith.

"I swear by Allah that this matter (Islam) will reach its perfection, so that a rider will go from San'a to Hadrmaut fearing nothing but Allah, the Almighty; or a wolf which may attack sheep; but you are in quite hurry." (Bukhari).

195. ***'Adi bin Hatim (r.a.) reports:***

"Once I was with the Holy Prophet (p.b.u.h.) that a man came to him and complained of his poverty. In the meantime another person came and complained to him of highway robbery.

Thereupon the Messenger of Allah turned toward me and said:

"Adi! Have you seen al-Hira? Thereafter he added:

"If you live long enough you will certainly see a woman travelling from al-Hira to go round the Ka'aba fearing none but Allah, the Almighty.

"If you live long enough, you will see that the treasures of Kisra (Chosroes) will be conquered.

"If you live long enough you will certainly see a man coming out with a handful of gold or silver looking for someone to accept it but he will find none to be accepting it from him.

"One of you will meet Almighty Allah on the appointed day when Allah will ask him: `Did I not send you a Messenger to convey My Message to you?"

"Certainly Yes," he will admit.

"Did I not give you property and show favour to you?" Allah, the Almighty will ask.

"Certainly yes," he will accept without any hesitation.

Thereafter the said: The person will look towards his right and he will find 'Hell,' then he will look towards his left and will see 'Hell.'

"Saying this, the Messenger of Allah warned: Guard against `Hell' even though it be with half a date, and if one can not get so much he should do it with a good word."

'Adi bin Hatim adds:

"I have seen a woman travelling from al-Hira to go round the Ka'aba fearing none but Allah, the Almighty.

I was among those who conquered the treasures of Kisra, son of Hurmuz; and if you will live long enough you will see what Abul QAsim (the Apostle) had foretold the third thing to happen." (Bukhari).

196. ***Hazrat Hudhaifa bin Al-Yaman reports:***

"The people would ask the Holy Prophet (p.b.u.h.) about good, but I used to ask him about evil fearing that it might overtake me. Once I submitted to the Apostle of Allah.

"O Prophet of Allah! We were in ignorance and in evil and Allah has bestowed upon us the present good; will there be any evil after this good?" "Yes." he replied.

"Will there be good after that evil?" I asked.

"Yes, but this good will be tainted with a little evil," he said.

"Yes, there will be some people who will invite others to the doors of Hell; and whoever accepts their invitation, will be thrown into it," he said.

"Describe those people to us," I asked.

"They will belong to us and speak our language," he said

"What do you ask me to do if such a thing should take place in my life," I asked.

"Adhere to the group of Muslims and their chief," he said.

"If there is neither a group (of Muslims) nor a chief (what shall I do)?" I asked.

"Keep away from all those different sects, even if you have to bite (i.e., eat) the root of a tree, till you meet Allah while you are still in that state." (Bukhari).

197. ***Hazrat Abu Sa'eed Khudri (r.a.) reports:***

"We were with the Prophet of Allah when he was distributing the booty. A man from Bani Tamim came to the Apostle and said:

"Act equitably, O Messenger of Allah!"

"Who will act equitably if I do not?" the Apostle said.

Thereupon Hazrat Umar (r.a.) sought permission to cut off his head.

"Leave him," said the Messenger of Allah and added;

"He is better than those who recite the Qur'an but it does not pass their collar bones. They deviate from the religion as an arrow goes through the animal aimed at. They will be recognised by the presence of a black man of whose upper arms quiver like a woman's breast, or like a piece of meat; and they will revolt against the best section of mankind."

After this Abu Sa'eed (r.a.) says:

"I testify that I heard this from the Messenger of Allah, and I testify that Ali bin Abu Talib (r.a.) fought with them and I was with him. He gave orders about that man who was sought for and when he was brought in, and I looked at him, he was exactly as the Prophet of Allah had described him.

198. ***In another version it is narrated:***

"A man with deep-set eyes, a projecting brow, a thick beard, high cheek bones and a shaven head came forward and said:

"Fear Allah, O Muhammad!"

"Who will obey Allah if I disobey him?" the Apostle replied and added, "Allah entrusted me with power over the inhabitants of the earth but you do not."

At this a man sought permission to kill him but the Apostle prevented him from doing so.

When the man turned away, the Messenger of Allah said:

"From this man's stock there will be people who recite the Qur'an, yet it will not pass their throats. They will swerve from Islam as an arrow goes through the animal shot at. They will kill the followers of Islam and leave the worshipers of idols alone; but if I live to their time I shall certainly kill them as Aad were killed." (Bukhari; Muslim).

199. ***Sa'eed bin Jaber (r.a.) reports from Hazrat Abdullah ibn Abbas (r.a.):***

"Umar bin Khattab (r.a.) had very sympathetic attitude with Abdullah ibn Abbas (r.a.) and treated him very favourably.

Once Abdul Rahman bin Auf (r.a.) said to him:

"We also have sons that are equal to him."

"It is because of his knowledge," Hazrat Umar (r.a.) replied.

Thereafter Umar (r.a.) asked Ibn Abbas to interpret the verse:

"When come the help of Allah and Victory."

"It portends the death of the Messenger of Allah," Ibn Abbas (r.a.) said.

Thereupon Hazrat Umar (r.a.) said:

"I do not know from this verse but what you know." (Bukhari)

200. ***Hazrat Abdullah bin Mas'ud (r.a.) reports:***

"Once Sa'd bin Mu'adh (r.a.) came to Mak'kah with the intention of performing `Umra. He stayed at the house of Umaiyya bin Khalaf, for Umaiyya himself would stay at S'ad's house whenever he passed by Madina on his way to "Shamm" (Syria).

When Sa'd (r.a.) wanted to go round the Ka'ba, Umaiyya said to him:

"Will you wait till mid-day when people leave for their homes so that you perform "Tawaf" round the Ka'ba peacefully."

But while Hazrat S'ad bin Mu'adh (r.a.) was going round the Ka'ba Abu Jahl turned up and asked:

"Who is there performing Tawaf?"

"I am S'ad," replied Hazrat S'ad Ibn Mu'adh (r.a.).

"Are you going round the Ka'aba, although you have given refuge to Muhammad and his companions?" Abu Jahl said.

"Yes" Sa'd replied.

Now they started quarreling. At this Umaiyya bin Khalaf came forward and said advising Sa'd:

"Don't shout al-Abi-I-Hakam (Abu Jahl), for he is the chief of the valley (of Mak'kah)."

Thereupon Sa'd told Abu Jahl:

"By Allah, if you prevent me from performing the `Tawaf' of the Ka'ba, I will spoil your trade with `Shaam."

But Umaiyya bin Khalaf kept on saying to Sa'd:

"Don't raise your voice," and took hold of him.

At this Sa'd grew furious and rebuked Umaiyya, saying:

"Be away from me, for I have heard the Prophet of Allah saying that he will kill you."

"Will he kill me?" Umayyia asked.

"Yes!" Sa'd said with confidence.

"By Allah, when Muhammad says a thing, he never tells a lie," Umayyia also said with certainty. Thereafter he went to his wife and told her:

"Do you know what my brother from Yathrib (Madina) has said to me?"

"What has he said?" she asked.

"He claims that he has heard Muhammad saying that he will kill me," he said to his wife.

"By Allah! Muhammad never tells a lie," she replied.

When the Mak'kan army proceeded towards Madina that resulted in the Battle of Badr, Umayyas's wife reminded him the prediction of the Apostle of Allah saying:

"Don't you remember what your brother from Yathrib had told you?"

Thereupon Umaiyya decided not to join the battle. But Abu Jahl persuaded him by saying:

"You are from the nobles of the valley (of Mak'kah), so you must accompany us for a day or two."

Thus very reluctantly Umaiyya bin Khalaf joined the battle and the prophecy of the Messenger of Allah came exactly true.

201. ***Anas bin Malik (r.a.) reports :***

"Once the Holy Prophet (p.b.u.h.) found Thabit bin Qais missing from his assembly. When he enquired about him a man said:

"O Messenger of Allah! I shall bring you his news."

So he went to Thabit and found him sitting in his house brooding his head in sadness.

"What's the matter?" the man asked Thabit.

"An evil situation!" replied Thabit and added.

"A man would raise his voice over the voice of the Prophet of Allah and so all his good deeds have been annulled and he is from the people of Hell."

The man went back to the Messenger of Allah and told him what Thabit had said.

Hearing the utterances of Thabit, the Apostle of Allah said:

"Go and say to Thabit:"You are not from the people of Fire; you are rather from the men of Paradise." (Bukhari).

202. ***Hazrat Abu Hurairah (r.a.) reports:***

"Once the Holy Prophet (p.b.u.h.) predicted: "This branch from Quraish will ruin the people."

"What do you enjoin us to do in such a case?" the Companions of the Messenger of Allah asked.

"I would ask you to keep away from such people," the Apostle of Allah said to his companions.

203. ***Sayeed Al-Umawi reports:***

"Once I was with Hazrat Abu Hurairah (r.a.) and Marwan and heard Abu Hurairah saying:

"I heard the most trustworthy (the Prophet) as saying:

"The destruction of my followers will be brought about by the youngesters from Quraish."

"Youngesters?" Marwan asked with wonder.

"If you wish, I would name them: They are the children of so and so and the children of so and so," Abu Hurairah replied confidently.

204. ***Believers will remain Victorious:***

Hazrat Abu Sayeed Al-Khudri (r.a.) reports:

"Once the Holy Prophet (p.b.u.h.) said: "A time will come the people (Muslims) will wage holy war, and it will be asked:

"Is there any amongst you who has enjoyed the company of Allah's Apostle?" They will say "yes" and then victory will be bestowed upon them.

"They will wage holy war again, but it will be asked:

"Is there any among you who has enjoyed the company of the Companions of Allah's Apostle?"

"Yes" they will say and then victory will be bestowed on them."

205. ***Hazrat Abdullah bin Umar (r.a.) reports:***

"The Jews will fight you, and you will be given victory over them.

That time even a stone will say:

"O Muslim: there is a Jew behind me; so kill him!" (Bukhari).

206. ***Hazrat Al-Mughira bin Shu'ba (r.a.) narrates:***

"Once the Holy Prophet (p.b.u.h.) said: "Some of my followers will remain on the right path and hence victorious till the Day of Resurrection."

207. ***Mu'awiya (r.a.) reports:***

"I heard the Holy Prophet (p.b.u.h.) say: "A group of people amongst my followers will remain obedient to Allah's orders and they will not be harmed by anyone. And they will remain victorious till the Last Day provided they remain obedient to Allah, the Almighty." (Bukhari).

208. ***Predictions Coming True:***

Abu Humaid al-Sayeedi reports:

"While accompanying the Holy Prophet (p.b.u.h.) on the expedition to Tabuk, we arrived at "Wadi al-Qura." While passing a garden belonging to a woman, the Messenger of Allah asked us to estimate its value. We did as ordered. Then the Prophet of Allah estimated it at ten camel loads. The Apostle then told the woman to calculate the value of her garden till we return, should Allah will.

Thereafter we left the place.

When we reached the Messenger of Allah told us: "You will have a violent storm tonight, so I tell you that nobody should get up till it is blowing and persons having camels must hobble them firmly."

As predicted by the Apostle of Allah, a violent wind started blowing, and as a man, ignoring the order of the Prophet, got up, and he was carried away by the strong wind and thrown between the two mountains of Tayy.

We then a came back and passed the garden at Wadi al-Qura.

When the Messenger of Allah asked the woman how much fruit her garden had amounted to, she replied:

"Ten camel loads!"

209. ***Unaisa, the daughter to Zaid bin Arqam reports on the authority of her father:***

"The Prophet (p.b.u.h.) went to visit Zaid when he was ill.

Consoling him the Prophet of Islam said to him:

"Your illness will bring about no harm to you," and "how will you do if your life is prolonged but you become blind?" "I shall seek my reward from Allah and show endurance," Zaid replied.

Thereupon the Messenger of Allah said to him:

"In that case you will enter paradise without being taken to account," the Prophet of Allah predicted (Bukhari).

210. ***Jabir (r.a.) reports:***

Once the Holy Prophet (p.b.u.h.) asked me, "Have you got carpets?"

"Wherefrom can we get carpets?" Jabir replied.

"But you shall soon have carpet?"

When my wife manged to have carpets, I used to say to her:

"Remove your carpets from my sight," but she would say in reply:

"Didn't the Prophet of Allah tell you that you would soon have carpets?"

Thereupon, I gave up asking her to do so.

211. ***Seeing the Useen:***

Hazrat Abdullah bin Umar (r.a.) reports:

"Once some Jews came to the Prophet of Allah and informed him that a man and woman from amongst them had committed adultery.

The Messenger of Allah asked them:

"What, according to Torah (Old Testament) is the legal punishment of illegal sexual intercourse?" "We announce their crime and lash them," the Jews replied.

"You are telling a lie; the Torah contains the order of "Rajm" (stoning), Abdullah bin Salam, a learned Jew turned Muslim said.

Thereupon, they brought the Torah and opening it placed their hand on the verse of "Rajm" and read the verses preceding and following it.

"Lift your hand," Abdullah bin Salam asked them.

When they lifted their hand, the Verse of "Rajm" was found written there.

"Muhammad has told the truth; certainy, the Torah has the Verse of 'Rajm'.

Thereafter the Holy Prophet (p.b.u.h.) issued order that the convicted should be stoned to death.

The order was implemented without loss of time. Abdullah bin Umar (r.a.) said:

"I saw the man leaning over the woman to shelter her from the stones." (Bukhari).

212. ***Hazrat Bara bin Azib (r.a.) reports:***

"A certain companion of the Holy Prophet (p.b.u.h.) recited Surah Kahaf in his prayer. A riding animal in the house got frightened and started jumping.

The person, while finishing his prayer, found something like cloud or mist hovering over him. When he informed the Apostle of Allah of the occurrence, the Apostle said:

"O so-and-so it (cloud or mist) was sign of peace descending for the recitation of Qur'an." (Bukhari).

213. ***Hazrat Abu Sayeed Khudri (*r.a.*) reports:***

"On a journey with the Holy Prophet (p.b.u.h.), we reached 'Usfan and passed some nights there. Some of us uttered that their stay there served no purpose, and their children were left unnoticed and unsafe. When the Messenger of Allah heard, he told:

"I swear by Him in whose hand my soul is that there is no ravine or mountain pass in Madina which does not have two angals on guard till your return (to Madina).

The Prophet of Allah then asked us to set out and we came back to Madina. Then, by Him in whose name oaths are taken, we had not yet unloaded our beasts after entering Madina that we were attacked by Banu Ghatfan.

214. ***Hazrat Abu Ayub Ansari (r.a.) reports:***

"Once on hearing a load sound the Holy Prophet (p.b.u.h.) came out; while the sun had already sat and he told us:

"The Jews are being punished in their graves." (Bukhari, Muslim)

215. ***Asim bin Kulaib reports from his father on the authority of an Ansar:***

"Once we accompanied the Holy Prophet (p.b.u.h.) to a funeral. On coming back from the graveyard, someone invited the Apostle on behalf of a widow. He accepted the invitation and we went for the feast alongwith him.

Food was served. We, alongwith the Messenger of Allah, put morsels of food in our mouths. We noticed that the Apostle of Allah was moving a morsel round in his mouth. Then he said:

"This flesh of a sheep has been taken without the permission of its owner."

When informed the woman sent her messenger to the Apostle who explained the matter on her behalf:

"Messenger of Allah: I sent to "an-Naqi" (a place where sheep were sold) to bring a sheep for the feast. But no sheep was available there. Thereafter, I sent a neighbour of mine to bring the sheep he had purchased for him and charge the price from me. But he did not turn up with the sheep. Later on, I sent another man to his wife who sent the sheep to me."

Hearing this the Messenger of Allah said:

"Give this food to the prisoners." (Abu Dawud; Baihaqi).

216. ***Dreams Coming True:***

Hazrat Abu Musa Ash'ari (r.a.) reports the Holy Prophet (p.b.u.h.) to have said:

"Once in a dream I saw migrating from Mak'kah to a place having plenty of date-palms. I thought that to be either Yamawa or

Hajar. But it was Madina (Yathrib). In the same dream I saw myself brandishing a sword and its blade got broken. It only symbolised our defeat in the Battle of Uhud. When I moved the sword again, it bacame normal as before and symbolised our final victory in the same battle." (Bukhari).

217. ***Hazrat Abdullah Ibn Abbas (r.a.) reports:***

"Once Musailma al-Kaz'zab (i.e., liar) came to Madina with his followers and said:

If Muhammad appoint me his successor. I am ready to follow him."

The Messenger of Allah went to him with Thabit bin Qais bin Shams. He then had a leaf of date-palm in his hand. Standing before Musailma and his followers, the Holy Prophet (p.b.u.h.) said:

"If you ask me even this piece of a leaf, I would not give it to you. And you can not save yourself from the wrath of Allah, the Almighty. If you reject Islam, Allah will destroy you. I think you are most probably the same person I have seen in my dream."

Later on Hadrat Abu Hurairah (r.a.) narrated to me that the Messenger of Allah told him:

"Once I was sleeping that I saw (in dream) two gold bracelets round my arm. I was too much worried at the sight. In the meantime, I was divinely instructed I should blow them off. I did according to the instruction, and both of them flew away.

Now I interpret the two bracelets as symbols of two liars who will claim prophethood after me."

This prophecy came true as Al-Ansi and Musailma Kaz'zab claimed prophethood.

218. ***Blessing Animals:***

Jarir (r.a.) narrates:

"Once the Holy Prophet (p.b.u.h.) said to me :

"Why do you not give me rest from Dhul Khalasa?" I replied him:

"I could certainly do it but I am unable to keep from falling off a horse's back.

Thereupon the Messenger of Allah gave me such a blow on my chest that I could see the mark of his hand on it and said:

"O Allah, make him sit firm and guide him to lead it (the horse) right."

Thereafter, I never fell off from my horse. And following this event, he left with one hundred and fifty horsemen and got victory.

219. ***Hazrat Anas (r.a.) reports:***

"Once there occured a great alarm in Madina so that the Companions of the Holy Prophet (p.b.u.h.) got embarressed. When the Messenger of Allah heard it, he came out at once, took a horse and left to enquire about the matter. The horse belonged to Abu Tala. It was a slow horse and took short steps.

Having returned, the Prophet of Allah said:

"I found this horse of yours running like a great river."

Thereafter no horse could compete with it in speed and no horse could ever outstrip it." (Bukhari).

220. ***Hazrat Jabir (r.a.) reports:***

"Once I accompanied the Holy Prophet (p.b.u.h.) to an expedition on a camel which was used for drawing water. It had grown weak and weary and could hardly go on. The Messenger of Allah came near me and asked what was the trouble with my camel. Thereupon the Prophet of Allah came behind my camel and urged it to go on fast and made supplication for the speed. The camel speeded up and outstripped all other camels. The Messenger of Allah asked me again how I found my camel: "It is fine now due to your blessing," I said to him.

"Would you sell it to me for an 'Uqiya'?" the Apostle asked me.

I agreed on condition that I might ride it till we come back to Madina. When we came back to Madina, I took the camel and appeared before the Prophet of Allah early next morning. He gave me the price of the camel fixed by him and then returned my camel to me too. (Bukhari; Muslim).

221. ***Sa'sa'a reports Abu Saeed Al-Khudri (r.a.) to have said:***

"I see that you love sheep and you keep them. Hence keep them well and take care of their food; for I have heard the Holy Prophet (p.b.u.h.) say:

"A time will come in the life of the Muslims that their best property will be their sheep. They will take this property of theirs to the tops of mountains and to the places of rainfalls in order to save their religion from afflictions." (Bukhari).

222. ***Urwah (r.a.) reports:***

"Once the Holy Prophet (p.b.u.h.) gave me one 'dinar' to buy a sheep for him. I brought two sheep for him with the money. Then I sold one of the two sheep for one dinar and brought one dinar and a sheep to the Messenger of Allah. Thereupon the Prophet of Allah blessed me in my deals. From that day on, I would gain even if I dealt in dust." (Bukhari).

223. ***Hazrat Abu Hurairah (r.a.) reports the Holy Prophet (p.b.u.h.) to have said:***

"A horse may be kept for one of the three purposes: for one it may be a source of reward; for another it may be a means of living; and for a third one it may be a burden.

As for the man for whom the horse is a source of reward, he is the one who keeps his horse for the sake of 'Jihad'. In Allah's cause; he ties it with a long rope in a pasture or in a garden. So whatever its rope allows it to graze, will become rewardable (for its owner).

A horse is an honest means of providing a livelihood which is right, legal and honest.

But the horse is a burden for those who use it for committing sins and earning illegal living. Moreover, if such a horse is kept for showing pride and for harming the Believers. (Bukhari).

224. ***Supplicating For A Mother:***

Hazrat Abu Hurairah (r.a.) reports:

"My mother was a polytheist and I used to ask her to accept Islam. Once I invited her to profess Islam, but she uttered such words for the Holy Prophet (p.b.u.h.) that I can not dare repeat them. However, I went weeping to the Messenger of Allah and requested him to supplicate Alimighty Allah to guide my mother. "O Allah, guide Abu Hurairah's mother," the Aposite said.

I rushed back home very cheerfully. When I reached my house I found the door shut. Having heard the sound of my feet, my mother said.

"Stay where you are, Abu Hurairah." I did accordingly. In the meantime, I heard splashing of water and thought she was taking bath. My notion was true. She finished her bath, put on her chemise and hurriedly opened the door to take me in.

As I came face to face with my mother, she spoke out with great zeal:

"I testify Abu Hurairah, that none has the right to be worshipped but Allah and I testify that Muhammad is His servant and Messenger."

In a fit of joy I turned back running to the Prophet of Allah with the good news of my mother accepting Islam, the Apostle praised Almighty Allah and uttered some good words." (Muslim).

225. ***Hazrat Abu Hurairah (r.a.) narrates:***

"You generally say that Abu Hurairah reports much more from the Holy Prophet (p.b.u.h.), but Allah, the Almighty knows the truth very well. My bretheren among the Emigrants (Muhajirin) would remain occupied with their business in the markets; and the Helpers (Ansar) are engaged with the affairs of their property. But I, being a poor man, had no other business other than keeping myself close to the Messenger of Allah and filling my stomach with what is available.

One day the Prophet of Allah rose to address us and said in the beginning: "No one among you who spreads his garment and keeps it so till I finish my address will ever forget to what I say."

Having heard the Apostle saying so, I spread my wollen garment till the Messenger of Allah finished his address. Thereafter, I gathered the garment and embraced it; and I swear by Him who sent him (the Apostle) with Truth that until this day I retain each word of his address (Bukhari; Muslim).

226. ***The Sick And The Possessed Cured:***

Hazrat Ya'la bin Murra Thaqafi (r.a.) reports:

Three things I have seen relating to the Holy Prophet (p.b.u.h.): once we were travelling with the Messenger of Islam that we passed a camel which on seeing the Apostle rumbled and kept its neck down. The Appostle of Allah stopped near it and asked about the owner of the camel. When he turned up, the Apostle asked him:

"Will you sell it to me?"

"No, I shall give it to you, Messenger of Allah" he said, and added, "It belongs to a family which has no other means of livelihood."

The Holy Prophet (p.b.u.h.) said:

"Since you have mentioned all this, note that it has complained to me of too much work and a very small amount of fodder; so treat it well and fear Allah, the Almighty."

Thereafter we proceeded till we came to a state that we needed rest. The Prophet of Allah lay down to have a sleep. All of a sudden a tree rushed towards the Prophet of Allah cleaving the earth till it overshadowed him and then it went back to its former place.

As the Apostle of Allah awoke I mentioned the matter to him.

Thereupon, the Apostle said:

"It is a tree which asked its Lord's permission to give me its salutation and He allowed it to do so."

We then travelled on till we passed a watering-place and there a woman brought her son who was possessed. The Prophet of Allah seized the nostril of the boy and said:

"Come out, for I am Muhammad, the Messenger of Allah."

On the return journey when we passed the watering-place the Apostle asked the woman about her son and she said:

"I swear by Him who appointed you with the Truth that no disturbing sign appeared since you left the place." (Sharh as-sunna).

227. ***Hazrat Abdullah ibn Abbas (R.A.) reports:***

"A woman brought her son to the Holy Prophet (p.b.u.h.) and said:

"O Messenger of Allah, my son is possessed, and it seizes him at morning and evening meals."

Hearing this the Prophet of Allah gave a blow to his breast and made a supplication and the possessed boy vomited some puppy-like object and got recovered," (Darimi).

228. ***Junaid bin Abdur Rahman reports:***

"I saw Sa'ib bin Yazid when he was ninety-four years old. He was then quite straight and strong. On enquiry he revelaled: "I know that I am enjoying good health, eye-sight and auditory power only because of the invocation of the Messenger of Allah. Once my aunt took me to him and entreated:

"O Prophet of Allah! my nephew is sick, so please invoke Allah for him. The Apostle of Allah, the Almighty, invoked and the result is before you." (Bukhari).

229. ***Hazrat Abdullah bin Abbas (r.a.) reports:***

"When the Holy Prophet (p.b.u.h.) visited a patient, he would console by saying:

"No harm will befall you! May Allah cure you! May Allah cure you!"

Once the Messenger of Allah visited a sick Bedouin and uttered the same words. Thereupon the Bedouin said:

"You say, may Allah cure me. But it is fever which boils in an old man."

"Then may it be so as you say." (Bukhari)

230. ***Wrath on Wrong-doers:***

Hazrat Salama bin Akwa (r.a.) reports:

"Once a man was eating with his left hand. When the Holy Prophet (p.b.u.h.) saw he said:

"Eat with your right hand."

"I am not able to do so," he replied with pride.

"May you not be able!" the Messenger of Allah said.

The man narrated that he could not raise his hand up to mouth from day that on. (Muslim).

231. ***Throwing out of A Dead Body By The Earth***

Hazrat Anas (r.a.) reports:

A Christian embraced Islam and would recite Surah al-Baqara and Ali-Imran. He also used to write the revelation for the Holy Prophet (p.b.u.h.).

Later on he reverted to Christianity and started saying:

"Muhammad knows nothing but what I have written for him." Then he died and was buried. But in the morning they found his body out of the grave. At this they blamed that this was done by Muhammad and his Companions. They have opened the grave of our companion and took out the body, because he had renounced their religion.

Hence they again dug a grave and got him buried in it. But the next morning they found to their wonder that the earth had thrown the body out. They again blamed Muhammad (p.b.u.h.) and his Companion for this. Thereafter, they dug a third grave as deep as they could and buried the body in it. But they found that the earth had once again thrown the body out.

Now they had to believe that the act was not performed by any man and hence they left the body unburied. (Bukhari).

232. ***Working Wonders:***

Hazrat Anas (r.a.) reports:

"Once, in a very dark night, Usaid bin Hudhari and Abbad bin Bishr was talking with the Holy Prophet (p.b.u.h.) till late. They took leave at the dead of night. The night was so dark that there was nothing visible. Both of them had a staff each in their hands.

As they proceeded on, the staff of one of them gave light enough to make the way quite visible. They went on witout any hinderence.

When their ways parted, the staff of the next one also produced light. Thus both of them reached their houses safe and sound.

233. ***Jabir (r.a.) reports:***

"Before the Battle of Uhud my father called me during the night and said:

"I feel that I shall be among the first of the Prophet's Companions to be killed, and after the Holy Prophet (p.b.u.h.), I love you most. I owe a debt; so pay it after I am no more and take care of your sisters."

The next morning he joined the battle and he was the first to be killed, and I buried him in a grave alongwith others.

234. ***Hazrat A'isha (r.a.) reports:***

"When Negus (Najashi), the king of Habsha (Abyssinia) died, they saw a light over his grave." (Abu Dawud).

235. ***Hazrat A'isha (r.a.) reports:***

"After the final departure of the Holy Prophet (p.b.u.h.), when the people wanted to wash his body a confusion arose over the manner of washing. They could not decide whether to strip the Apostle of his clothes as it is done with others or to wash with his clothes on. When they could not agree, Allah, the Almighty cast sleep on them, so that everybody's chin was on his breast. Then someone whose identity could not be known, addressed them from the corner of the house saying:

"Wash the Prophet with his clothes on."

So they got up at once and washed the Messenger of Allah with his clothes on: pouring water over the shirt and rubbing the body with the shirt." (Baihaqi).

236. ***Ibn al-Munkadir (r.a.) reports:***

"Once Safina, the client of the Holy Prophet (p.b.u.h.) missed the Islamic army in the land of the Byzantines. He was anxiously running from pillar to post in search of the army. On his way, he came across a lion and addressing it he said:

"I am the client of the Messenger of Allah and I am now victim of such and such circumstances."

Thereupon, the lion came forward wagging its till and guided me along the way tail I joined the army. The lion then went back."(Sharh Sunna).

237. ***Abu Khaleda reports:***

"Once I asked Abu Aliya whether he had heard anything from Anas about the saying of the Holy Prophet (p.b.u.h.) and he (Anas) said:

"I served the Messenger of Allah for ten years without a break and had his utmost blessings all these days. My garden would produce two crops of fruit every year; and a basin in the garden would give off odour of 'musk'.

238. ***Urwa bin Zubair reports:***

"Arwa, the daughter of Aus brought a dispute against Saeed bin Zaid bin Amr bin Naufal before Marwan bin Hakam. She claimed that he had grabbed a piece of her land. Saeed said:

"Would I take any piece of land belonging to her after what I heard from the Holy Prophet (p.b.u.h.)?"

"What have you heard from the Prophet of Allah?" he was asked. Thereupon he said that he had heard the Apostle say:

"If anybody grabs a piece of land, it will be tied round his neck like a necklace."

"I shall ask you nothing after what you said," Marwan told Saeed.

"O'Allah! If she is lying, make her blind and kill her in her land," Saeed cursed her.

She lost her eyesight and died falling into a hole in her land." (Bukhari, Muslim).

239. ***Hazrat Abdullah bin Umar (r.a.) reports:***

Hazrat Umar bin Khattab (r.a.) appointed a man named Sariya as commander of the Islamic army.

After some days, Hazrat Umar (r.a.) was addressing the Believers from the pulpit of the Mosque of the Prophet. All of a sudden he shouted at the top of his voice:

"O Sariya! keep near the mountain!"

A messenger from the army came later to Madina and told the Caliphh of Islam with wonder:

"O Commander of the Faithful! We met our enemy and they were about to rout us that someone cautioned us by shouting loudly:

"Keep near the mountain, Sariya!"

Hearing that call, we set our back to the mountain and routed the invading army." (Baihaqi).

240. ***Uqba bin Amir (r.a.) reports:***

"The Holy Prophet (p.b.u.h.) prayed for the martyrs of the Battle of Uhud eight years after the battle. He prayed in a manner as if he was bidding farewell to the living and the dead. He then mounted the pulpit and said:

"I am one to go before you and I shall be a witness against you. Your appointed place is the Pond (of Kauthar) I am looking for. I do not fear that you will turn polytheists after I am gone, but I am afraid you will plunge into worldly comforts and perish like your predecessors." (Bukhari, Muslim)

241. ***Hazrat A'isha (r.a.) reports:***

"One of Allah's favours to me was that the Messenger of Allah passed away in my house and that he joined his saliva with that of mine when he died.

During his last hours, my brother, Abdur Rahman bin Abu Bakr, came in with a tooth-stick in his hand. The Holy Prophet (p.b.u.h.) looked at it. I knew that he liked to brush his teeth with it. When I asked him if he wanted to have it, he nodded his assent. I gave it to him. But it proved too hard for him. So I asked him if I could soften it, and he nodded his assent. I softened by chewing it and then he moved it over his teeth. There was a jug of water in front of him and he began to put his hands into the water and wiped his face with them, saying meanwhile: "None has the right to be worshipped but Allah. Death has pang." Then he raised his hand and said:

"(Put me) with the Highest Companion!" till his hands dropped." (Bukhari).

242. ***Hazrat A'isha (r.a.) reports:***

I heard the Holy Prophet (p.b.u.h.) say:

"No Prophet suffers from any illness unless he is given a choice between this world and the next one."

The Messenger of Allah, during his last illness, suffered from severe hoarseness, and I heard him say:

"(Keep me) with those of Prophets, upright, martyrs and pious ones to whom you have shown your favour. Now one may infer from these words that the Last Prophet (p.b.u.h.) was also given a choice." (Bukhari, Muslim).

243. ***Hazrat Anas (r.a.) reports:***

"When the Holy Prophet (p.b.u.h.) fell ill, he was found anxious. Thereupon Fatima (r.a.) expressed her grief by saying:

"Alas for the anxiety, my father!"

"Your father will have no anxiety after today," the Apostle said.

"O my father! You have responded to a Lord who summoned you. O my father! Your destination is the Garden of Paradise."

When the Messenger of Allah was laid to rest and Hazrat Anas (R.A.) came back, Fatima (R.A.) said addressing him:

"Anas, have you people found it an easy task to scatter dust over the Prophet of Allah?" (Bukhari).

244. ***Hazrat Anas (r.a.) reports:***

"When the Holy Prophet (p.b.u.h.) came to Madina there was alround happiness. The Abyssinians played with their spears of joy. Abu Dawud transmitted it.

Darimi transmits him saying: I have never seen a brighter day than the day the Apostle of Allah arrived in Madina; and I have never seen a darker day than the day on which Allah's Messenger passed away.

245. ***Hazrat A'isha (r.a.) reports:***

"When the Holy Prophet (p.b.u.h.) passed away, there was difference of opinion among the Companions regarding his place of burial. Thereupon Abu Bakr (r.a.) said:

"A Prophet is laid to rest at a place he passes away." Thereupon, the Messenger of Allah was buried at the place he passed away. (Tirmidhi).

246. ***Hazrat A'isha (r.a.) reports:***

"The Holy Prophet (p.b.u.h.) used to say, when he was well and good, that no Prophet leaves this world unless his resting-place in paradise is shown to him, and a choice is given to him.

She further narrates:

"When death approached the Messenger of Allah, he had his head on my thigh and he fainted. When he regained his consciousness, he stared at the ceiling and uttered:

"O Allah! (put me) with the Highest Companion." (Bukhari, Muslim).

247. ***Hazrat A'isha (r.a.) reports:***

During his last illness, the Holy Prophet (p.b.u.h.) said:

"A'isha, I still feel the pain from the food I ate at Khaibar. (Bukhari).

248. ***Hazrat Abdullah Ibn Abbas (r.a.) reports:***

"When the last moments of life drew near, the Holy Prophet (p.b.u.h.) asked those present to bring pen and paper and write a document so that you will not deviate from the right path after I am gone."

Umar Ibn Khattab (r.a.) who was also present there, stopped people from doing so as the pain was supposed to have overpowered the Apostle. He further said that the Book of Allah (Qur'an) was enough for you.

But the people in the house got divided and a section rose in favour of getting document written by the Messenger of Allah.

But when clamour and confusion prevailed, the Prophet of Allah said to the people.

"Get up and leave me."

Ubaidullah reports Abbas to have said:

"It was a terrible calamity which intervened to prevent the Messenger of Allah from writing a document for us owing to disagreement and clamour."

Sufyan reports from Sulaiman to have heard from Abbas:

The prophet of Allah later gave three commands:

"Expel the polytheists from Arabia and keep rewarding the deputations."

As to the third command he reports:

"The Apostle of Allah either did not mention it or I had forgotten it." (Bukhari; Muslim).

249. ***Hazrat Anas (r.a.) reports:***

After the demise of the Prophet (p.b.u.h.), Hazrat Abu Bakr (r.a.) said to Hazrat Umar (r.a.),

"Come and let us visit Umm Aiman (r.a.) as the Messenger of Allah would do."

When the two great Companions of the Apostle came to her, she burst into tears."

"What makes you weep," they asked.

"I am not weeping because of the final departure of the Prophet of Allah; for what lies with Allah, the Almighty is better for the Apostle of Allah. I am, rather, weeping that the process of Revelation has now ceased."

This statement of Umm Aiman (r.a.) stirred the visitors and they also joined her in shedding tears." (Muslim).

250. ***Hazrat A'isha (r.a.) reports:***

Once I said, "O my head!" The Holy Prophet (p.b.u.h.) heard and said "If you were to die while I am alive I would ask forgiveness for you and make supplication on your behalf." Thereupon I said:

"Alas! I swear by Allah that I think you want me to die; and if that happened you would spend that night with one of your wives."

Following this, the Messenger of Allah smiled, and thereafter, the pain that caused death to the Apostle began to be felt. (Bukhari; Darimi).

251. ***Hazrat Abu Musa Ash'ari (r.a.) reports:***

Once the Holy Prophet (p.b.u.h.) said:

"When Allah, the Almighty means mercy to a people He causes the Prophet of the time to die and makes him (the Prophet) a forerunner who goes before them. But when He means death and destruction to a people causes it during the very lifetime of the Prophet so that the Prophet gets comforted and satisfied that the disbelievers are suitably punished." (Muslim).

252. ***Hazrat Abu Hurairah (r.a.) reports:***

Once the Holy Prophet (p.b.u.h.) said:

Even if the 'Deen' (religion) would be found hanging with the 'Suraiyya' (cluster of seven brilliant stars in Taurus), some people of Persia would get it." (Sahihain).

This saying of the Holy Prophet (p.b.u.h.) refers to men of wisdom and learning like Hazrat Imam Abu Haneefa and Hazrat Imam Bukhari and many others who served Islam at all levels.

253. ***Once the Holy Prophet (p.b.u.h.) said:***

"Very soon people will make long journey in search of knowledge, but none will be found greater than the scholar of Madina." (Hakim).

According to Sufyan bin Ayyiah, the scholar of Madina referred to by the Messenger of Allah was Hazrat Imam Malik.

254. ***Hazrat Abdullah Ibn Mas'ood (r.a.) reports:***

Once the Holy Prophet (p.b.u.h.) said:

"A great scholar will be born among the Quraish and will fill the earth with the treasures of knowledge." (Abu Dawud).

The above saying of the Messenger of Allah has also been reported by Hazrat Ali (r.a.) and Hazrat Abdullah Ibn Abbas (r.a.) and is quoted in Baihaqi.

This prediction came true in the form of Hazrat Imam Shafei who was born among the Quraish and was the greatest scholar ever born among them. He was among the offsprings of Muttalib Ibn Abd Munaf.

255. ***Imam Ahmed and Abu Dawud quote from Hazrat Abdullah bin Umar (r.a.).***

Once the Holy Prophet (p.b.u.h.) said:

"A section of my Ummah will be called Qadriya and it will be like a Magi (a fire-worshipper)."

This saying of the Messenger of Allah is also being quoted by Tabrani from Hazrat Anas (r.a.).

Qadriya is a sect which believes that all power rests with men and God has no business to interfere with. Thus God is helpless and worthless and men are powerful in all spheres of life.

256. ***Imam Mustaghfari reports from an authentic narrator in 'Dalail-e-Nabviya.'***

The narrator puts:

"We three persons were going to Yemen. A man from Kufa was with us. He was reproaching Hazrat Abu Bakr and Hazrat Umar. We tried to stop him and ask him not to use filthy language against the great Companions of the Messenger of Allah. But he did not pay any heed to our advice. Now it was night. We lay down to sleep at a place near Yemen. At dawn, we performed ablutions and awakened that person too. Having awakened from sleep, he said regretfully that alas, he would not be able to accompany them any further. It is because I saw in dream that the Apostle of Allah was standing at the head of my bedstead and saying:

"O transgressor! Your face will get deformed just over here."

However, we asked the 'Kufi' to get up and wash his face. But when he rolled his legs together, his fingers showed sign of changes. In a short while both his legs looked monkey-like and gradually the whole body turned into a monkey.

At last we tied him with our camel and left. We reached a forest before sunset. There were a few monkeys in the forest. When the 'Kufi monkey' saw them he broke the string and mixed up with them.

257. ***Imam Mustaghfari narrates:***

"A virtuous man reported that a man from Kufa accompained me in journey. He used to reproach Hazrat Abu Bakr and Hazrat Umar (r.a.). We tried our best to prevent him from doing so, but he did not pay any heed. At last we excluded him from our company and left.

On our return journey, we met his slave and enquired about his master and told him to tell him to accompany us home.

The slave informed us that his master had undergone a wonderful change; both of his hands have turned like a pig.

Hearing this we went to the 'Kufi' and asked him to accompany us home. Thereupon, he replied that he has suffered something very precarious. Saying this, he took out his hands which resembled like a pig. In the way there was a group of pigs. The Kufi could not resist his tempetation and jumped down from the mount and mixed up with them."

258. ***Abu Dawud, Tirmidhi and Hakim report the Holy Prophet (p.b.u.h.) to have said:***

"In near future my Ummah will be divided into 73 sects, and all but one, will go to Hell."

Thereupon the Companions of the Holy Prophet (p.b.u.h.) asked.

"Which are the people that are destined to enter Paradise?"

"Those who will follow me and my Companions" the Messenger of Allah said."

The prophecy made by the Prophet of Allah in this saying has already come true. After the pious Caliphates, the people differed with respect to creeds and Rawafiz, Khawarij, Muntazila, Jabriya, etc., came into existence. Their number at last, reached 73. And among them there is only one to go to Heaven because they follow the path of the Holy Prophet (p.b.u.h.) and his Companions.

259. ***Hazrat As'ma bint Abu Bakr (r.a.) reports the Holy Prophet (p.b.u.h.) to have said:***

"Banu Thaqeef will produce one beast and one liar." (Muslim).

The above prophecy came true. The blood-shedder born to

Banu Thaqeef was Hajjaj bin Yusuf. His blood-thirstiness knew no bounds and volumes had been written on his love for shedding blood. Tirmidhi reports on the authority of Hisham bin Hibban that he got killed one lakh twenty thousand persons without any considerable fault.

Another man belonging to Banu Thaqeef who was declared as liar by the Messenger of Allah was Mukhtar Thaqafi. He was a great liar and imposter. He claimed to be the successor of Imam Muhammad Hanafiah; earned name and fame by circulating his claim to avenge the martyrdom of Imam Husain; and at last claimed his own prophethood. (Muslim).

260. ***Hakim, Baihaqi and Abu Naeem report the Holy Prophet (p.b.u.h.) to have said about Thabit bin Qais (r.a.):***

"O Thabit! you will remain alive commendably and you will die as a martyr."

The above prophecy came true as Hazrat Thabit (r.a.) was killed in the battle of Yamama fighting Musailma Kaz'zab during the Caliphate of Hazrat Abu Bakr (r.a.).

261. ***Hazrat Abu Zar (r.a.) reports the Holy Prophet (p.b.u.h.) to have said addressing him:***

"Once Madina will see carnage on such a large scale that blood will stick to the black stones and will not remain visible."

This prophecy came true when the Madinites refrained from Yazeed after the martyrdom of Imam Husain. Yazeed sent a bloody expedition to Madina under the charge of Musrif bin Uqba. A bloody fight took place at Harra where black stones were lying. Hundreds of the Companions of the Holy Prophet (p.b.u.h.) and their offsprings were killed and black stones were covered with human blood.

262. ***Hazrat Raji bin Khadeej (r.a.) reports the Holy prophet (p.b.u.h.) to have said in an assembly:***

"In this assembly of yours there is one whose tooth-jaw will be like that of Uhud mountain in the Hell."

Hazrat Abu Hurairah (r.a.) narrates that all those present in that assembly, except two, passed away. That I am one of the two; and the next one was killed in the battle of Yamama.

Thus the prophecy of the Prophet of Allah regarding a man in that assembly came true.

263. ***Baihaqi reports:***

"When the death period of Hazrat Abu Zar (r.a.) drew near, his wife began to weep because her husband was dying at Rabza where there was nothing except forests. There was none to get him shrouded and buried.

Hazrat Abu Zar (r.a.) asked his wife not to shed tears as the Messenger of Allah had told an assembly, and I was also present there, that one of you will die at a place where there will be no population; and a band of Muslims will arrive at the spot. I think I am the person who was referred to here."

Thereafter he asked his wife to go out and wait on the way.

She narrates:

"When I went out I saw some persons approaching. I narrated to them all about Abu Zar (r.a.). Hearing this they came to Abu Zar (r.a.). He told them:

"Provide for me a shroud belonging neither to a Government official nor of a wealthy person."

Hearing this a young man advanced and said:

"My uncle! I give you my trousers-string and two pieces of cloth for shroud. These articles have been woven by the yarns spun by my mother."

Abu Zar (r.a.) accepted the shroud and when he died he was washed and buried after prayer was led for him. Thus the prophecy of the Apostle came true.

264. ***Tabarani and Baihaqi report from Ibn Hakeem Ghabti:***

"When Abu Hurairah (r.a.) would meet me he would ask about the well-being of Hazrat Sumra bin Jundab (r.a.). When I would say.

"Sumra is well and good," Abu Hurairah would express his joy.

One day I asked Abu Hurairah (r.a.):

"Why do you ask about the well-being of Sumra every now and then?"

Abu Hurairah (r.a.) replied:

"Once we ten persons were assembled in a house. On that occasion the Holy Prophet (p.b.u.h.) said:

"Among you ten men the one who dies last will be in the fire."

Thereafter Abu Hurairah (r.a.) added:

"Eight out of ten persons have already died. Now only Sumra and I are alive. Thus if Sumara dies before me, I shall be left for the fire."

Abu Hurairah (r.a.) was frightened that even if someone would tell him out of joke that Sumra had died, he would get fainted. At last he died before Sumra.

But the fear of Abu Hurairah (r.a.) was based on a misunderstanding.

Ibn Asakar reports from Ibn Sirin that Samra had a disease which caused biting cold. Hence he would sit on a cauldron containing boiling water in it, for getting himself warmed. One day, while doing the same excercise he fell down into the cauldron and died.

By the Prophecy, the Messenger of Allah did not mean Fire of Hell; what he meant was the fire of this world only. Thus his prophecy came true.

265. ***Bukhari and Muslim report from Hazrat Abu Saeed Khudri (r.a.) that the Holy Prophet (p.b.u.h.) said:***

"You will follow in the footsteps of those who have passed before you." The Companions asked:

"Do you mean the Jews and Christians from our predecessors?" "Yes, who else then," the Apostle replied.

266. Now the Prophecy of the Messenger of Allah for the Muslims has come true as they have started aping the Jews and the Christians in traits and character, manners and conduct. Jealousy; hiding the truth; interpreting the verses wrongly for worldly gains, etc., were the ways of the Jews. While the Christians used to raise their Prophet and saints to the Divinity.

Each of the traits mentioned above is found among the Muslims of the present age.

266. ***Tabarani, Darqitni and Baihaqi report that addressing Hazrat Abdullah bin Zubair (r.a.), the Holy Prophet (p.b.u.h.) said:***

"You will suffer from others and others from you."

This prophecy of the Messenger of Allah came true. Hazrat Abdullah bin Zubair (r.a.) bacame Caliph in 64 A.H. after the martyrdom of Imam Husain. All Islamic countries except Syria recognised his Caliphate.

In 73 A.H. Abdul Malik bin Marwan sent a large expedition against Hazrat Abdullah bin Zubair (r.a.). The army surrounded Mak'kah and killed Abdullah bin Zubair. Thus the Caliph suffered. And since the followers of the Caliph were killed in large number, Kabah was stoned because of the house of the Caliph lying in the vicinity of the Ka'abah. Moreover, his killers were liable to be thrown into the Hell.

267. ***Baihaqi and Ibn Adi report the Holy Prophet (p.b.u.h.) to have said about Zaid bin Sujan:***

"One of his organs will reach the Heaven before all others."

This prophecy came true as some historians had written that his left hand was cut off from his body in the battle of Nahawand.

268. ***Baihaqi and Hakim report from Hasan bin Muhammad that the Holy Prophet (p.b.u.h.) said to Hazrat Umar (r.a.):***

"I hope Suhail bin Amr will do something to make you feel gratified."

It is said that when the sad news at the demise of the Messenger of Allah reached Mak'kah, the followers of the Apostle felt extrmely disturbed and they might deviate from the path of Islam. But the fiery speeches of Suhail bin Amr kept them away from leaving the path of Islam. Thus the prophecy made by the Prophet of Allah came true.

269. ***Imam Ahmed from Abdullah bin Abbas (r.a.) and Hakim and Baihaqi report from Hazrat A'isha (r.a.) that Abbas bin Abdul***

Muttalib was captured in the Battle of Badr and brought to Madina. On that occasion a particualr amount was fixed as ransom for the release of the captives:

Abbas, the uncle who was also among the Captives of Badr, appeared before the Holy Prophet (p.b.u.h.) and submitted:

"The amount of ransom fixed for my release is not available with me; how then I can produce so heavy an amount."

Thereupon, the Messenger of Allah turned towards Abbas and said:

"What happened to your wealth deposited with Umm Fazl with the will that in case of your being killed your wealth will get divided among your offsprings."

At this revelation of the fact, Abbas got embarrassed and said to the Prophet:

"How did you come to know this for nobody knew about the wealth except Umm Fazl and myself." Thereafter Abbas paid the ransom from the money brought from Umm Fazl.

270. ***Baihaqee reports from Hazrat Urwah (r.a.):***

"Once a dromedary of the Holy Prophet (p.b.u.h.) was lost and could not be found out inspite of tremendous searching.

Thereupon a hypocrite tauntingly said:

"Muhammad (p.b.u.h.) claims to reveal the unknown things; why the bringer of revelation does not reveal the whereabout of the lost dromedary."

Thereupon Hazrat Jibrail came and informed about the taunting of the hypocrite and trace of the lost dromedary.

Thereafter, the Messenger of Allah came out and said:

"I don't claim to know the hidden facts, but my Lord has disclosed to me about the taunting of the hypocrite as well as the lost dromedary. My dromedary is there in so and so ravine and her bridle has got entangled with a tree."

Hearing this, the Companions of the Prophet of Allah rushed towards the ravine and found the lost dromedary in a state described by him.

271. ***Ibn Asakar reports from Wathila bin Athqa:***

"Once I appeared before the Holy Prophet (p.b.u.h.) and found him sitting in the assembly of his Companions. I sat in the middle of the circle. The Companions of the Apostle asked me not to do so. Thereupon the Messenger of Allah said to his Companions:

'Let him sit here, for I know his intention."

"Tell me O Prophet of Allah as to why have I come to you?" Wathila asked.

"You have come to know about the difference between "Certainty" and "Uncertainty," the Apostle explained. "Yes, O Messenger of Allah, I have come to know exactly what you said.

Thereupon, the Apostle of Allah further said:

'Certainty' is one which sticks to heart and which satisfies the heart of a Believer. "Uncertainty" is that which does not satisfy the heart. Hence you should do what looks "certain" and avoid what looks "uncertain."

272. ***Baihaqee reports from Abu Bardah bin Neyaz (r.a.):***

"I brought three cut off heads before the Holy Prophet (p.b.u.h.) and said:

"I have killed the two but fail to know who has killed the third one. I have only seen that a tall and fair-complexioned person has killed him and I have only lifted his head."

Thereupon the Holy Prophet (p.b.u.h.) said:

"So and so angel has killed him."

273. ***Baihaqee reports from Sa'b bin Abi Habeesh who had come to fight the Believers in the Battle of Badr. He narrates:***

"By Allah I also ran away when the Quraish took to their heels. No one captured me. But all of a sudden a tall and fair-complexioned person appeared sitting on horse between heaven and earth. He tied me up and left there. In the meantime, Abdur Rahman bin Auf came. He saw me tied up and asked the soldiers as to who had tied him up. But nobody claimed to have tied him up. He brought me to the Prophet of Allah.

"Who has tied you up?" asked the Apostle.

"I do not recognise the person who has tied me up," I replied; and did not narrate what had happened because its mention meant confessing the truth of Islam and the existence of the angels. But hearing all this, the Messenger of Allah said:

"You have been tied up by an angel."

274. ***Imam Ahmed, Ibn Sa'd and Ibn Jarir (r.a.) report from Abdullah Ibn Abbas and Baihaqee from Hazrat Ali (R.A.):***

"In the Battle of Badr Abul Al-Yaser had arrested Abbas although the former was a very weak person and the latter was a very strong man.

The Holy Prophet (p.b.u.h.) once asked Abul Al-Yaser as to how he was able to capture Abbas. At this Abul Al-Yaser replied:

"A certain person I had never come across before helped me in tying him up."

"It was a very respectable angel who helped you in tying him," the Apostle explained.

275. ***Muslim reports from Hazrat Abu Hurairah (r.a.):***

Once Abu Jahl said:

"By Lat and Uzza, if I found Muhammad rubbing his nose on the ground, I shall trample his neck by my feet.

One day the Holy Prophet (p.b.u.h.) was saying prayer. Abu Jahl saw and got up in order to fulfil his design. But he retreated awefully as if anything was resisting him.

When the people asked what happened to him, he narrated:

"I saw between Muhammad and I a blazing trench and a very terrible scene and also some feathers."

Thereupon, the Messneger of Allah said:

"If Abu Jahl would come near me, the angels could tear him into pieces."

274. ***Sahihain report from Hazrat Abu Saeed Khudri (r.a.):***

"One night Hazrat Usaid bin Huzair (r.a.) was reciting Surah al-Baqara. His horse standing nearlly started jumping and tossing. As Usaid stopped the recital, the horse also became peaceful. And as he started reciting the Qur'an again, the horse started jumping once again. Usaid kept quiet again and the horse did it again. The excercise was repeated for the third time.

After saying his prayer, Usaid bin Huzair took aside his son, Yahya who was sleeping near the horse for fear of being trampled by the horse.

He then raised his eyes towards the sky and saw something spread like a canopy and display of lights in it. The next morning, he narrated the whole episode to the Messenger of Allah. Thereupon the Prophet of Allah said twice:

"Go on reciting the Qur'an."

Thereupon, Ibn Huzair submitted:

"O Messenger of Allah! I was afraid that Yahya might be trampled upon. And when I went near Yahya I saw a canopy which went on up and up and gradually it vanished.

The Apostle of Allah said to Usaid:

"Do you know what was that?

"No, O Messenger of Allah," Usaid replied.

"They were angels. They came near you because of your recital of the Qur'an. When you stopped the recital, they disappeared. Had you been reciting till the morning, the people would have seen them in the morning."

277. ***Baihaqee reports:***

"Once during the childhood, Hanzla bin Hazeem came to the Holy Prophet with his father and the Apostle had spread his hand over his head and supplicated for his well-being. As a result of this whenever a man had his mouth or a she-goat had its udder swollen, got cured after being touched by the head of Hanzla.

278. ***Tabarani reports:***

"When Ayed bin Amr received injury in the Battle of Hunain, the Holy Prophet (p.b.u.h.) cleansed his blood and invoked blessings of Allah for him. As a result of this, his forehead always kept shining.

279. ***Baihaqee reports from Amr bin Tholeba Jahni (r.a.):***

"I met the Holy Prophet (p.b.u.h.) at SeYala and embraced Islam on the spot. The Prophet of Allah spread his hands on my face and head."

As a result of this, Tholeba died at the age of 100 and the hairs of his head and beard touched by the Apostle of Allah never grew white till his death.

280. ***Ibn Abdul Barr reports in Al-Istiab:***

"Once the Holy Prophet (p.b.u.h.) was taking bath that his daughter Zainab came across. He sprinkled a little water on her face. As a result of this, her face looked fresh and shining till her old age.

281. ***Tabarani reports from Abu Amama:***

"Once the Holy Prophet (p.b.u.h.) was taking his meal. In the meantime a young girl turned up and asked for some food. The Apostle of Allah gave some food from his dish. But she requested that she wanted to have food from his mouth. The Prophet of Allah took out some food from his mouth and gave it to her. The girl ate it up.

It is said that the girl was notoriously shameless in the whole Madina, but after eating from the food of the Apostle, she came to be known as the most shameful woman of Madina.

282. ***Baihaqee reports:***

With the blessings of the Holy Prophet (p.b.u.h.), Abdur Rahman bin Auf (r.a.) grew very rich. He hoped to find gold even if he removed a stone from its place. He had gold in his house so much in quantity that after his death during the Caliphate of Hazrat Uthman Ghani (r.a.), it was cut into pieces by an axe and the cutters would get tired.

He had four wives. He divorced one of his wives during his last illness. And she was given one -fourth of the eighth part of the whole property and it amounted to eighty thousand dinars to which she agreed.

Moreover, Hazrat Abdur Rahman bin Auf (r.a.) had made a will to give away fifty thousand dinars in the way of Allah. He also donated a garden of four lakh rupees to the holy wives of the Holy Prophet (p.b.u.h.) and gave away lakhs of dinars as alms, charity etc.

283. ***Baihaqee reports in Dalail-e-Nabuwah:***

"Once the Holy Prophet (p.b.u.h.) supplicated for Abu Qatadah (r.a.) in the following words:

"May your face have success and well-being; and O Allah! bless the hairs and the body of Abu Qatadah."

"As a result of this supplication Abu Qatadah (r.a.) died at the age of 70, without a single hair being white; and his face looked like that of a boy of 15.

284. ***Tirmidhi and Baihaqee report:***

The Holy Prophet (p.b.u.h.) supplicated for Sa'd bin Abi Waq'qas (r.a.) in the following words:

"O' Allah, accept the supplications of Sa'd."

As a result of this supplication every supplication of Hazrat Sa'd bin Abi Waq'qas (r.a.) was accepted by Allah, the Almighty.

285. ***Sahihain report from Hazrat Abdullah Ibn Abbas (r.a.):***

"O Allah! Confer upon Ibn Abbas knowledge and understanding of Islam and that of commentary of the Holy Qur'an."

As a result of this supplication, Abdullah Ibn Abbas (r.a.) used to be called "a man of deep learning" and the "Interpreter of Qur'an."

286. ***Bukhari, Dareqatni and Imam Ahmed report:***

The Holy Prophet (p.b.u.h.) invoked blessings for Urwah. He narrates:

"As a result of this supplication I would, by Allah, return from the market of Kufa getting not less than a profit of forty thousand."

As per Bukhari Urwa profitted from even by purchasing soil.

287. ***Baihaqee and Ibn Majah report:***

"Once the Holy Prophet (p.b.u.h.) invoked:

"O Allah! Save Ali from the rigours of cold and heat."

As a result of this Hazrat Ali (r.a.) used to wear warm clothes during summer and thin clothes during winter.

288. ***Baihaqee reports from Imran bin Haseen:***

"One day I was at the service of the Holy Prophet (p.b.u.h.) that his younger daughter Hazrat Fatima (r.a.) came in. Her face had turned pale because of hunger.

The Messenger of Allah put his hand at the chest of Fatima and supplicated:

"O filler of the hungry and lifter of the fallen, raise Fatima, the daughter of Muhammad and remove her misery."

I saw that her face began to shine and paleness disappeared. From that day on she never felt hungry.

289. ***Khatib reports:***

"A person belonging to Yamama brought his oneday child to the Holy Prophet (p.b.u.h.) on the day of Hajjatul-wida'a. The Prophet of Allah asked that child of oneday.

"Who am I?"

"You are the Prophet of Allah (peace be upon you)."

"You are telling the truth," the Messenger of Allah said and added, "May Allah bless you."

From that day on, the child never uttered a word unless he attained an age when a child starts speaking.

290. ***Muslim reports from Asma'a bint Abu Bakr (r.a.):***

She took out a robe and said:

"This robe was worn by the Holy Prophet (p.b.u.h.) and wherever water after washing this robe was made to drink a patient he would get cured."

291. ***Tabarani reports from Hazrat Abu Hurairah (r.a.):***

"Once Hazrat Husain (r.a.) was crying for water. The Holy Prophet (p.b.u.h.) put his tongue in his mouth and the thirst was quenched and he stopped crying."

292. ***Baihaqee reports in Dalail-e Nabuwah and Ibn Barr in al-Istiab from Umm Aasim, the wife of Utbah bin Farqad (r.a.):***

"We three were the wives of Utbah (r.a.) and we used best of the perfumes. But the fragrance coming out of the body of Utbah excelled all of us. One day I asked Utbah about the secret of his odour. He narrated:

"Once I fell sick. The Holy Prophet (p.b.u.h.) came to me and having got me undressed, took his saliva; rubbed it on his palms and spread it on my belly and back. And from that day on, my body produces such a fragrance that all others are subdued by it."

293. ***Tabarani and Baihaqee report:***

"Sherjeel Jafi (r.a.) had developed hard lumps in his palm so that he could not catch hold of a sword nor could he hold the rein of the horse. When the Holy Prophet (p.b.u.h.) came to know, he pressed his hand and the lumps were cured.

294. ***Baihaqee reports:***

Once Hakam bin Abi-Aas was sitting in the assembly of the Holy Prophet (p.b.u.h.); and when the Apostle would utter anything he would cause convulsive motion in his face and make signs towards the hypocrites with the intention of ridiculing the Apostle.

Seeing this the Messenger of Allah said:

"May you be so!"

As a result of this curse he would cause convulsive motion in his face the whole life.

295. ***Baihaqee reports from Asma'a bint Abu Bakr (r.a.):***

"When the wife of Abu Lahab came to know about the revelation of Surah Lahab, she took a stone and came to hurl it at the Holy Prophet (p.b.u.h.) who was sitting in the mosque with Abu Bakr (r.a.).

But when she came near only Abu Bakr (r.a.) was visible. She turned blind for the Apostle. She saw here and there and went back saying:

"I have heard Muhammad using bad words for me; had I found him, I would have hurled this stone at him."

296. ***Baihaqee reports from Osama bin Zaid (r.a.):***

"Once the Holy Prophet (p.b.u.h.) said:

"One who attaches anything wrong to me will find his place in the Hell."

Once the Messenger of Allah sent someone somewhere. He attached something wrong to the Apostle and circulated it to the people.

When the Prophet of Allah came to know about this, he cursed him. As a result of this, his stomach got burst after death and the earth threw him out."

297. ***Ahmed and Bizar report from Anas bin Malik:***

"Once the Holy Prophet (p.b.u.h.) accompanied by Hazrat Abu Bakr, Hazrat Umar and an Ansari entered a garden. There were some she-goats. They lay in prostration before the Prophet of Allah.

Thereupon Hazrat Abu Bakr (r.a.) submitted:

"It is more obligatory on us to bow down before you."

"None is liable to be worshipped but Allah," the Apostle said.

298. ***Muslim and Abu Dawud report from Abdullah bin Jafar (r.a.):***

"Once the Holy Prophet (p.b.u.h.) entered a garden. There was a wicked camel and would bit the entrants.

The Messenger of Allah called him. He came near and lay down in prostration before him; and then sat nearby. Then the Apostle said addressing the camels:

"All except the wicked jinn and men know that I am the Prophet of Allah.

299. ***Tabarani and Baihaqee report from Umm Salma (r.a.):***

"Once the Holy Prophet (p.b.u.h.) was passing through a forest that a doe called him. A villager was sleeping nearby. The Prophet of Allah asked:

"What do you want to say?" "This villager has captured me and two kids of mine are lying hungry in a ravine. If you set me free I shall come back after suckling them," the doe said.

"Will you really come back?" the Apostle asked.

"Yes," she replied confidently.

The Prophet of Allah released her. She came back after suckling her kids. The Apostle tied her up.

When the villager got up he asked the Apostle as to what did he want?

"Set her free," the Prophet of Allah advised him. She left saying:

"I bear witness that there is none worthy of worship and you are the Prophet of Allah."

300. ***Abu Yala and Tabarani report from Hasan:***

"When Halima Sa'dia carried Muhammad (p.b.u.h.) for suckling it proved to be a blessing for her.

It was a period of scarcity because of famine. Even pastures were dried up. There was want of grass. In such a case goats used to come back home hungry and weary. But even in such a situation, the goats of Halima would return eating to the fill, fresh and happy.

THE END

INDEX

A

D

E

F

H

R

S

U

W

Y

Z

* * * * *

It also analyses the Quranic evaluation of the beliefs and moral values of other ancient peoples, like the Jews and the Christians, and comments on the modern philosophic concepts of Marx, Toynbee and Spengler.

Demy 8vo **pp 246** **1994** **Rs. 125/-**
ISBN 81-7435-007-1

QUOTATIONS FROM THE HOLY BOOK

Obaid Qadri

The Holy Qur'an is the record of Divine revelations directly communicated to the Holy Prophet of Islam. The teachings of Islam are meant not for Muslims but for all mankind to follow. It is with this objective in view that this short collection of quotations has been prepared.

Demy 8vo **pp vii+86** **1994** **Rs. 30/-**
ISBN 81-7435-20-9

THE QUR'ANIC CONCEPT OF WAR

Brig. S.K. Malik

It is perhaps the first and only book of its kind in which Qur'anic philosophy of war has been analysed from a technical and professional point of view.

Demy 8vo **pp XXX+159+10Maps** **1992** **Rs. 125/-**

INTRODUCTION TO QUR'AN

Dr. Hafiz Muhammad Adil

M.A., LL.B, Ph.D.

This is an introduction to the Holy Book-Al Qur'an in a simple language specially meant for the young generation. Text of some selected suras with transliteration, translation and simple commentary has been given.

Demy 8vo **pp VII+140** **3rd Edition 1994** **Rs. 50/-**

A DICTIONARY AND GLOSSARY OF THE KORAN

John Penrice

This work has been compiled with the intention of its proving of service to the beginner in mastering some inevitable difficulties, and also to the more advanced Arabic in resolving some problems. Thus it provides a clue of elucidation to the more intricate passages of the Quran: it is also an indispensable aid to Quranic studies.

4TO **pp V+166** **1991** **Rs.175/-**

INDEX-CUM-CONCORDANCE FOR THE HOLY QUR'AN

Al-Haaj Altaf Ahmed Kherie

The Holy Qu'ran is divided into various chapters, each dealing with one particular subject. It is difficult for an ordinary person to look up any particular subject or point easily. For instance, Hadrat Musa is mentioned at 136 different places in 34 suras: and there are a large number of verses in which his name is not mentioned but which relate to him.

So, the Author decided, each and every verse of the Holy Qu'ran could be properly and systematicaly indexed, subject wise, to make easy to any person to look up any particular verse that he wished to consult.

4TO **pp L+(43)+a-z+1116** **1992** **Rs.550/-**

QUR'ANIC STORIES SERIES

A. Hussain

This is a series of seven small books for children. All stories are taken from the Holy Qur'an. These stories are "the accommodated path" to build up the Islamic character in the life of Muslim children.

1. The First Man 2. Man of The Cave 3. Trenches of Fire 4. Army of Elephants 5. People of Sabbat 6. Owners of The Garden 7. Three True Believers.

Royal 8vo **2nd Edn. 1994** **Rs. 70/-Set**

REVELATION AND REVOLUTION IN ISLAM

Prof. Zia-ul-Haque

This book discusses the lives missions, characters roles struggles and achievements of the Prophet revolutionaries of Islam. These men appeared in pre-capitalist times to liberate humanity from the yoke of oppression and slavery. The author focuses on the nature of Prophethood, revelation and revolution. He answers the following questions: What is truth? What is the social significance of the religious conception of revelatory truth? What is the difference between revelatory truth, Revolutionary principle and ritual?

The Prophet revolutionaries discussed in the book are Nuh, Hud, Salih,

Ibrahim, Shuayb, Musa, Isa and Muhammad. These men fought against the community of oppressors, the Quran Zalima, and guided, mobilized and organized the rebels, the poor and the weak and led the struggles to establish an egalitarian social order in society.

pp vi+258 1992 Rs. 90/-

MOSES V/S PHARAOH

A. Hussain

A detailed, comprehensive narration of the grand and heroic struggle launched by Prophet Moses(PBUH) against Pharaoh. The great liberation movement of the downtrodden against a tyrant ruler has been presented, based on Quranic verses. A Guide for those who are fighting against the evil forces.

pp 144 2nd Edn. 1994 Rs. 50/-

SAHIH MUSLIM (4 VOLS.)

M. Abdul Hamid Siddiqi, Tr.

The first ever attempt at the English translation with Arabic Text with exhaustive notes and Commentary based on authentic Original sources and brief biographical Sketches of Major Hadith-narrators.

The most distinguishing feature of the translation and the explanatory notes of this work is that the translator has taken great care to adhire to the path of the old Orthodox Scholars has at the same time tried to incorporate the Modern Researches in different fields of knowledge which are valid from the Islamic point of view. This work thus combines in itself the authenticity and the correctness of old scholarship and the freshness of the modern style.

pp 3600 1996 Rs. 1250/-

MOHAMMAD IN WORLD SCRIPTURES

Abdul Haque Vidyarthi

This is the first book of its kind, containing prophecies about the advent of the Holy Prophet in the various scripturesof the world. It gives those prophecies in the original words of those scriptures. A great and quite original research work

pp X+242 1992 Rs. 125/-